The Secret War Factory

Cowbridge Confidential

by
Charles Exton

authorHOUSE®

AuthorHouse™ UK Ltd.
500 Avebury Boulevard
Central Milton Keynes, MK9 2BE
www.authorhouse.co.uk
Phone: 08001974150

2007 Charles Exton. All rights reserved.

No part of this book may be reproduced, stored in a retrieval system, or transmitted by any means without the written permission of the author.

First published by AuthorHouse 12/5/2007

ISBN: 978-1-4343-0224-3 (sc)

Printed in the United States of America
Bloomington, Indiana

This book is printed on acid-free paper.

Contents

Acknowledgments vii

Preface ix

Chapter 1 Just Me 1

Chapter 2 Setting the Scene, Living in the 30s 5

Chapter 3 Setting the Scene, Living during the War ... 11

Chapter 4 Early Days 21

Chapter 5 The Factory, First Impressions 31

Chapter 6 The Effects upon the Local Population 37

Chapter 7 Life in the Machine Shop 43

Chapter 8 Machine Shop Difficulties 59

Chapter 9 The Main Assembly Department 63

Chapter 10 Test and Inspection 77

Chapter 11 Further Problems 83

Chapter 12 The Coil Winding Department 89

Chapter 13 Other Departments 93

Chapter 14 Security 97

Chapter 15 The Home Guard Unit 101

Chapter 16 The Canteen 105

Chapter 17 Leisure Time 109

Chapter 18 The New Centimetric Airborne Radar ... 115

Chapter 19 Finale 123

Chapter 20 Bits and Pieces 127

Appendix Now it can be told 139
Abbreviations 153
Definitions 155
References 157

Acknowledgments

I would like to thank Chris Poole for his considerable help with the editing of this book. I am also grateful to Phil Judkins and Colin Latham for their help and advice. My family and friends showed considerable patience and support.

Preface

I should perhaps explain how I have such an in depth knowledge of the factory. On my arrival I was astonished at the attitude of the local people. I was more intrigued than annoyed and I decided to keep a diary, which I subsequently maintained. In those days I had many girl friends, not difficult with less than 100 men and over 900 girls! Their main topic of conversation was moans about their work, which the majority most heartily disliked as most were not there by their own choice. They hated the twelve-hour working day and were always looking for a shoulder to cry on.

When I was first directed to the factory I spent six weeks in all the production departments, i.e. the Machine Shop, Main Assembly and Coil Winding Departments, etc., so that I had a good experience of the overall operation before working in the Test Department. I was then moved to the Test Apparatus Department designing and building the specialised testing apparatus required. I was then loaned to the Coil Winding Department and ran the Test Department there. Later, when there were production problems there a night shift was started, and I was asked to manage that. For a while I managed the production Planning Department. Finally I became Chief Estimator negotiating Contract Costs with the Technical Cost branch of the Ministry of Supply. Therefore I had a good knowledge of the whole factory; consequently I had a better insight of the whole operation and a greater in depth appreciation of the problems than most other people.

In order to confirm as many facts as I could I spent a great deal of time at the Public Records Office studying the relevant files and a great deal of correspondence between E.K.Cole and various Ministries. I have also included excerpts from the Mass Observation Report, "War Factory" published in 1942, where appropriate.

The quality of some of the photographs leaves something to be desired, but remember these are amateur snapshots surreptitiously taken over sixty years ago.

Chapter 1
Just Me

I lived with my parents and sister on the outskirts of a city in the West Country. We had a large back garden that opened on to fields and then down to a river. As a small boy in the long summer holidays when the sun seemed to shine every day, I spent pretty well all of my time out of doors in the garden or out in the fields with my dog. I think I knew the names of all the birds, trees and wild flowers. On some days I went fishing or swimming in the river. My dog Jess loved the water and would swim with me, but would try and climb up on my back whilst I was swimming leaving me with nasty scratches. Sometimes the whole family would go swimming in the river.

I struggled with my eleven plus examination but I passed and won a scholarship to the Grammar School which was about two miles away and as a reward my father bought me a new bicycle. When I was about thirteen my father purchased a radio, or wireless set, as it was then known. I was most fascinated by this and wanted to know more about it. I was given a magazine "Wireless World" or "Wireless Companion" or something like that and learned a lot about wireless sets and was determined to build my own. It took several weeks' pocket money to save up enough to buy all the components but build the set I did and it worked! Whilst the family was downstairs listening to the wireless I was up in my room with the headphones clamped to my ears listening as well. Broadcasting was so different then. It started at 10am with a church service followed by music and talks. At 5pm was Children's Hour, and at 9pm the News and the close down. On Saturdays at 8pm there was a Variety Programme with singers, comedians etc. Learning about wireless made me realise that education was important and I started to take school more seriously and worked very hard at it.

I left Grammar School with passes in English, Maths, Physics and Chemistry and went to Technical College. The College had a wireless club that I joined enthusiastically and was soon given the job of running it. I spent several evenings a week building bigger and better wireless sets, as there were many components available. I also repaired many sets for the school staff and others. My course at the college finished at the end of September 1939. I was considering my future career, although the wireless industry never occurred to me as a career because that was my hobby. My first love was chemistry and I thought I should try for an apprenticeship with a chemical manufacturer, continue studying and become a qualified Industrial Chemist.

However, World War II had started and new rules and regulations were coming in thick and fast, among these were the Control of Labour Orders. I was ordered to attend an interview at the local Labour Exchange, (the local offices of the Ministry of Labour). There were many forms to be filled in with details of my education, hobbies etc and details of what I wanted to do and how I saw my future. I was told that I would be called back for another interview but if I wanted to take some temporary work in the meantime I could do so. It was six weeks or more before I was called again for an interview. I was told that due to the present circumstance I would not be able to follow a career in the chemical industry and that I was to join E.K.Cole at their new electronics factory in a large country house near Malmesbury, where I would be employed as an instrument maker. I told the interviewer that this was not what I wanted at all, to which he categorically replied that I had little option.

The Secret War Factory

"What none at all" I asked. "Well, there is always the army," he said.

In January 1940 I set off for Malmesbury and was met at the station from where I was taken to Cowbridge House about two miles from the town centre. I was photographed, rather like a criminal, and had many forms to be filled in again. I was told I would be issued with a Works Pass with my photograph in it and would not be able to enter the factory premises without it and I was to work in various production departments for a number of weeks before taking up a technical position and I would then be subject to the Official Secrets Act.

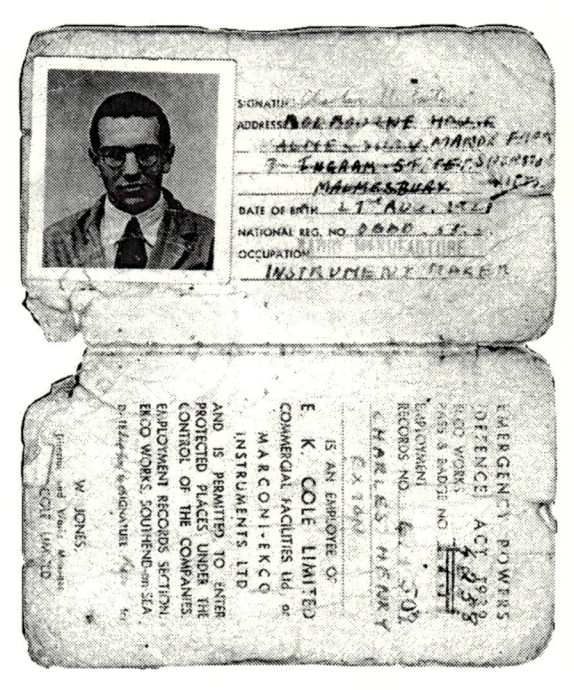

My well-worn works pass also showing my various wartime address's

Chapter 2
Setting the Scene, Living in the 30s

A generation is now growing up without relatives who lived through the Second World War. No-one under 70 now alive has any memories of War, always excepting our Armed Forces; so it may help my readers if I try to describe life in the 30s first of all, and then what living in a war felt like.

To get back to the 30s you have to try to picture a very different world. No computers, no mobile phones – very few telephones at all – no television, just a few radios. No washing machines or tumble driers. .No frozen foods and no refrigerators, except for the wealthy. Very few motor cars - the doctor had one and a telephone, but both of these possessions were way beyond the means and aspirations of the average working man. In many areas there was no electricity, and street lighting, such as it was, was gas. A man came round at dusk and turned each lamp on individually and they were all turned off at midnight. The lights in the home were gas, paraffin/oil lamps or candles. Houses themselves were a lot barer than today's and darker – not a lot of furniture, and paint and wallpaper were generally dark. Lights were generally one in a room: one bathroom in a house and many houses with no bathroom at all. In the kitchen, very few of today's appliances – just a sink. a coal fired range to cook on, a table and a couple of chairs.

The roads were much quieter than today. Most of the traffic was commercial, lorries and vans with a lot of horse drawn carts. Throughout the country there were only about 100,000 motor cars on the roads. Compare this with today's twenty million. In the countryside away from the towns, the roads were largely made of stone and dirt. There were men known as roadmen, or length men, who were each allocated a mile or so of road. They had a small hut for shelter where they kept their tools and a large supply of stones. It was their job to fill all pot holes and to ensure the roads were free of loose material and that the surface was kept in good condition.

You probably guess that the way we spent our time was quite different from today. It took a great deal longer to do things like prepare a meal, because you had to light a coal fire to heat up the oven in the range. Cleaning the house took longer with more coal dust about and no vacuum cleaners. Going shopping took longer – no supermarkets - so you had to go separately to the butcher, the baker, the grocer, the greengrocer, the fishmonger and so on. In the evenings time was spent reading, for those with that ability, or playing games. Very few had a radio set and broadcasting was very limited with very little choice of programme.

The most popular form of entertainment was going to the cinema (no television) and queuing to get in was quite common. Performances were at set times not continuous showing as today. Even the smallest town had a cinema and many changed their programmes twice a week. By 1944 cinema audiences rose to 25 – 30 million a week. Before the war cinemas were never opened on a Sunday. Listening to the Radio was becoming more popular as more and more people had radio sets and television was still very much in its infancy and only available in a part of

The Secret War Factory

the London area. On September 1st 1939 the BBC announced a single wartime channel of radio programmes and the television channel closed down altogether.

One other thing you'd probably notice was that everybody dressed much more warmly – no central heating! – but in rather drab clothes compared to today's - no dry cleaning either -, and the way people treated each other was different. Today we are used to treating people as equals, and questioning why people in authority do what they do. Before the war this was almost unknown – if someone in authority, say a policeman or a doctor told you to do something, you did it and you didn't ask why; you just assumed they had that right or they knew better.

In the north of the country coal mining, steel making, shipbuilding, and heavy engineering along with agriculture were the main employers of labour. In the south, building, light engineering and the newer manufacturing industries of motor cars and radio sets accounted for most employees. Women worked largely on shops and offices. Call centres and similar services of today were unknown before the WW2 war. In rural areas a very common job was being in 'domestic service' that is working in one of the many large country houses as cooks, general housework and waiting at table. It was not unusual for a large country house to employ up to 40, mostly women, in this capacity. In general married women simply did not work. In fact if a young woman worked in the Civil Service and became married she had to leave the work. The Civil Service did not employ married women.

The prolonged World Depression of the 30s caused considerable unemployment that peaked in 1932 to over three and a quarter million and by the outbreak of war in 1939 there was still over one and a quarter million unemployed. There was a great deal of poverty and it was surprising and wonderful in the way those in poverty helped each other. If one family had a loaf of bread and his neighbour had none then he would cut his loaf in half and give it to his neighbour. It was the oldest industries, shipbuilding, steelmaking and heavy engineering that suffered unemployment most. Tyneside, West Cumberland, Lancashire and much of South Wales became designated Distressed Areas. A certain amount of Government help was given to Distressed Areas. The 'Daily Telegraph' sponsored a scheme in the winter of 1936, which comprised of sending a Christmas Present by post, anonymously, to the children of every unemployed parent in the Distressed Areas. Every Department of State involved co-operated in the scheme. Six big London Stores were selected to send the gifts at an average price of 2s – 6d (12 ½ p). The girls worked voluntarily after hours to pack them. The stores themselves contributed money, as did many eminent people. King Edward VIII sent a cheque.

The distress in the South of the country was not so great and newer manufacturing industries had started up. However, they were not without their problems. The motor car factories in Coventry and Oxford laid off most of their workers during the winter months as during the summer they had produced sufficient cars to meet that years sales which took place, largely, during the spring and summer. The radio set manufacturers' were similarly affected but the other way round. They manufactured Radio Sets during winter when sales were greatest and laid off workers during the summer months. The girls living in Southend-on-Sea, where the Ekco Radio factory was located, had the best of both worlds. They worked at the Ekco factory during the winter months and in the summer worked in the many cafes and ice cream parlours, which only opened in the summer season.

By the mid 30s there was considerable unrest in Europe. Germany started a re-armament programme, which included a massive Air Force. In 1936 Civil War broke out in Spain. Our cinema newsreel programmes were showing pictures of Spanish towns being destroyed by German Bomber Aircraft who were supporting Franco's fascists in the Spanish Civil War. Whilst most people thought this appalling but it was largely put down to 'foreigners' antics.

The Air Ministry was more concerned and remembered WW1 when German Zeppelins made 20 bombing raids over London killing several people and destroying buildings. The RAF flew 81 sorties to try and intercept them but only made 3 sightings and failed to engage the enemy at all. This, when Zeppelins were 600 ft. long and travelled at 60 mph. They knew we had no defence against any incoming enemy aircraft. At that time there was talk of a 'Death Ray' and the Air Ministry offered a reward of £1.000 for anyone who could demonstrate a Ray that could kill a sheep at 100 yards! However, the Radio Research Laboratory suggested that it may be possible to locate flying aircraft using Radio Waves. Successful experiments were carried out to prove the idea and the Air Ministry awarded contracts to develop equipment, but under the utmost secrecy.

The sheer drudgery of life in the late 1930s has been overshadowed by the additional privations of the preparations for war. In 1938 tens of thousands of volunteers, more women than men, were in the Auxiliary Fire Service, as Wardens in Air Raid Precautions, or with the Women's Voluntary Service. The WVS organised the first evacuation of children away from cities at high risk from bombing in October 1938 and 38 million gas masks had been distributed. Terms and conditions were announced for ARP workers, women working full time were paid £2 a week; male workers £3 a week. Uniforms for both sexes were to comprise of an armband and a tin hat with ARP stencilled on the front, and special clothing and equipment for those dealing with gas. From 1941 a more practical heavy battledress uniform was issued. One and a half million volunteered for work in Civil Defence (over one million were unpaid).

Charles Exton

In April 1939 the Military Training Act conscripted all men of 20 and 21 years of age to compulsory military training. The Emergency Powers Act of August concluded the Defence regulations that were to dominate civilian life for the next 6 years. Everyone had to register and Identity Cards were issued and these had to be carried at all times. All road signposts and street name boards were to be removed to confuse any invaders. Church bells were silenced except to announce the landing of the enemy. The Government had made bales of cotton blackout material available at about 2s. a yard. Blackout curtains had to be fitted to all windows and doors. Families could be fined if any light glimmered from their windows. Torches had to be masked as did head lights on motor vehicles and thick white lines were painted on pavement kerbs. Women stuck tapes on their glass window panes so they would not shatter and faced their gloomy interiors with even more economical amounts of light, heat and comfort.

Places of public entertainment, cinemas, theatres, football grounds or mass meetings were immediately closed 'until further notice' to prevent large numbers of people being killed (They reopened in December 1939). Newspapers and trunk calls were censored and appeals made to limit telephone calls and post to a minimum.

On August 31st 1939, giving only 24 hours notice, the Government ordered the evacuation of children. On 1st September members of the WVS were ready at dawn to organise the evacuation of 1.5 million people which included 827, 000 unaccompanied children, 524,000 mothers and children under 5 years old, 13,000 pregnant women, 7,000 disabled people with 103,000 escorts. The Government had expected to evacuate about 4.5 million, but about 2 million people had evacuated themselves, and about 1 million refused to go.

Chapter 3
Setting the Scene, Living during the War

On Sunday 3rd September 1939 at 11.15am the Prime Minister Neville Chamberlain announced that we were at war with Germany. The following day National Services (Armed Services) made all men between 18 and 41 liable for conscription. Men in 'Reserved Occupations' escaped service in the Forces altogether, although they were liable to be directed into particular jobs. Limitations were put on what manufacturers could produce; raw materials were issued on a quota basis; production was 'zoned' to save transport costs, so what was available might depend on where you lived; permits had to be obtained in order to buy furniture. Parts of the country were out of bounds, as well as the beaches along the south coast. Mail was censored: letters were opened and anything that might be helpful to the enemy – details of a soldier's whereabouts that might suggest a troop build-up in a certain area, or the location of factories involved in war production – was removed.

Petrol Rationing began on 22nd September 1939. Coupons were issued; the value depending upon the horsepower of the car. This allowed for 200 miles motoring a month, but this allowance was not for long and then there was no petrol at all for private cars. Petrol was only allocated for vehicles used for essential purposes. Private cars, which had to be laid up, had to be made immobile by the removal of the carburettor or parts of the ignition system. Train services were much more extensive than they are today. Even large villages had a station, some on branch lines from the main network. Buses also had more extensive routes. Even so, both services were badly disrupted by the war. The movement of troops and war supplies taking priority and further disruption to the railways was caused by bombing. The locomotives of trains travelling at night of necessity had to open the fire doors at times to stoke the fire with coal. When this happened a wide beam of firelight was cast upon the blacked out countryside, which made a ready target for bombs and gunfire from enemy aircraft.

Announcements warned that food rationing was to come and in November 1939 people were ordered to register with the shops of their choice – butcher, grocer and dairy – and the housewife was thus introduced to what became a way of life for the next 15 years. From 8th January 1940 the shopper was limited to 4oz (114 gms) a week of ham or bacon, 12oz (340 gms) a week of sugar, and 4oz (114 gms) a week of butter per person. By March 1940 meat was rationed to 1s 10d (9p) worth a week later reduced to 1s 1d (5½ p) worth. Offal was not included and liver became a rare treat. By July 1940 the tea ration was reduced to 2oz (57 gms) a week and margarine, butter, cooking fats and suet were limited to about 2oz (57 gms) each a week. In March 1941 jam, syrup, and marmalade, followed by honey and lemon curd were put on coupons at between 8oz (227 gms) and 2lb (0.9 Kg) a month. In July of that year cheese was rationed at a pitiful 1oz (28 gms) a week although, like eggs, milk and fruit, the amount varied with the season.

Basic food rationing varied during the war according to supply and production. The range was 1s. (5p) to 2s 2d (11p) worth of meat, 4 – 8 oz (114 - 227 gms) of bacon, 1 – 8 oz (28 – 227 gms) of cheese, 1 – 8oz (3 – 24 gms) of fat, ½ - 2 eggs a week. ½

- 2 pints (½ - 1 Lt) of milk, 2 – 4 oz (28 – 114 gms) of tea and 8 – 16oz (227 – 454 gms) of sugar (increased during the jam making season). Sweets and chocolate fluctuated at 3 – 4 oz (85 – 142 gms), while soap eventually became a serious problem at 4oz (114 grms) a month. One tin of National Milk (four pints) (2¼ Lts) was permitted every four weeks and every eight weeks the bonus of an extra 12 eggs was allowed in the form of a packet of 'dried eggs'. This was a yellow powder which when mixed with water was supposed to give you the ingredients for scrambled eggs or for making a cake. Some people liked it; many did not! Fish was never rationed but was in such short supply that it became a rare treat. Bread was not rationed either, but the only bread available was the National Loaf made from 'national flour' (that is using nearly all the wheat including the husk) which made the loaf a dirty beige colour and heavy in texture. Fancy breads were prohibited.

Britain could only produce 40% of its food requirements, and the rest had to be imported. Wheat was imported from Canada and many other food products came from the U.S.A. The docks at London, Southampton, Liverpool and Bristol employed thousands of dockers who were engaged in loading and unloading the holds of these vast ships. This was a labour intensive operation men were literally carrying sacks of produce on their backs into and out of the ship's holds. The container ships of today were unknown before the war. This is how so much of our food arrived. So much shipping was lost due to enemy action – U boats and bombing – that food economies were essential. By April 1941 700,000 tons of shipping had been sunk. This is why food was rationed so severely.

Clothing rationing started in June 1941, all clothing was rationed except industrial overalls and hats. Every civilian was issued with 66 coupons a year. A mans suit took 26 coupons, a shirt 5, socks 3 (maximum length 7 ½ inches) shoes 7, a tie 1. Vest and pants took 8 leaving 16 that could be used for handkerchiefs at 1 coupon each, pyjamas or a dressing gown each of which took 8. A woman's suit or outdoor coat was 18 coupons; an unlined mackintosh was 9, a dress 11 if it was made of wool or 7 if it was made of cotton or rayon or some other fabric. Blouses and jumpers were 5 each, shoes 5 (but went up to7) a pair of stockings 2, vests and knickers 3 each, bras and suspender belts one each. Pregnant women were given first 50 then 60 coupons to buy maternity clothes and then a layette. In 1943 the coupon allowance was reduced from 66 to only 40 a year.

There were queues everywhere. Most people seeing a queue joined it, only knowing what they were queuing for when they got to the head of the queue. Shopping took so much longer then and everything was in short supply. The housewife's task became very difficult and the stressful pre-war life, so far away now, was good by comparison. Before the war a typical family was happily married with two small boys, the youngest of which had just started school. They lived in a small rented house in south London. What became of them? The two boys had been evacuated to somewhere in Somerset. The mother received letters occasionally from the eldest boy who had obviously written what someone else had told him. Her husband had been called up into the army and she had no idea where he was or what he was doing as his letters home were heavily censored. She herself had to work in a nearby factory and she bravely struggled with rationing, for one person, putting up the blackout every evening and keeping the home in good shape waiting for better times.

After December 1941, women and widows without children could be conscripted under the National Service Acts for the Armed Forces. However, the only women not required to register for employment in April 1941 were those already doing essential jobs: the Nursing Services, the Woman's Land Army or working in factories. The only 'mobile' women exempted from transfer away from home were those living with their husbands or married to servicemen. If a 'mobile' woman refused to be transferred to work away from home she could be 'formally directed' under the (Defence) Regulations 58A.

Munitions factories were often in remote districts for security reasons. Many eligible women were sent to them – in the words of the regulations 'to districts where labour is scarce in relation to demands for war factories'. Defence Regulations 1941 stated that anybody who tried to avoid direction, or left a job for a more congenial one, could be fined up to £5 a day 'while the default continued'. In practice it was known that the girls so fined just did not have the money to pay so instead they were transferred to one of the Armed Forces, from which there was no escape! However, at least one girl was imprisoned. Fines and imprisonment were imposed with severity by the courts. The exacting Security Regulations made everything from feeding birds with breadcrumbs, for which a fine of 40s (£2) could be imposed and chatting about a partner's whereabouts was also a fineable offence.

Women accordingly enrolled for work until almost all were doing war work. Such was the climate of opinion that many of the remainder volunteered to work from home at night, without pay if necessary. By 1942 32,000 people had been compulsory directed to work. The figure rose to 1 million by 1945. Even in1943 90% of single women and 80% of married women with children over 14 were working. Now, even groups classified as 'immobile' (i.e. those born before 1896 or those with children under 14) were exhorted to join the factories for a part time week of up to 30 hours, eventually even those in wheelchairs, the deaf, the blind and the old were being given work they could manage. Boys and Girls aged 16 – 18 were also required to register. Every man was required but not all went into the

Armed Forces. 30,000 were sent to work in the coal mines, as every ton of coal was desperately needed.

On 10th June 1940 Mussolini declared war on the allies. On 19th June the Germans marched into Paris and an armistice between France and Germany was signed on 22nd June. *Britain was left to fight alone.* The Germans were all over France, even in Calais, just a hop across the channel from Dover. German invasion into this country seemed inevitable. In case this happened and the Germans captured the BBC all newsreaders began their broadcasts by identifying themselves, for example 'here is the news and this is Frank Phillips reading it'. We were soon able to name all the newsreaders by their voices.

The first bombing raid on London took place in August 1940. Britain's Bomber Command retaliated by dropping bombs on Berlin. This infuriated Hitler because he had assured the people of Berlin that it would never be bombed. The war on capital cities had begun. Many people who had remained at home now felt it was time, or were compelled by the bombing, to move away. All those living in the country or other safe areas did not suffer from the bombs but they were all visited by the Evacuation Officer. He examined your home and if he thought you had enough room for one or more lodgers, then, one or more evacuees you had to have. This meant accommodating, feeding and generally looking after total strangers whether you liked the look of them or not, and all for 25 shillings a week (£1 – 25).

Early bombing raids were made on Tyneside, and then from 28th August for four nights Merseyside was the target. Large parts of Liverpool were completely burned out. Most of the early bombs, however, were dropped in the London area, the worst damage being suffered by Croydon, the City and the East End. In June about 100 civilians were killed; in July 300; in August 1,150. The next phase began on the night of 7th

September with a devastating raid on the dockland area. For 76 consecutive nights after, with an average of 200 aircraft, the Luftwaffe bombed London. The Docks and East End, the most densely populated area of London bore the brunt of these raids. On the peak bombing, 538 tons of bombs were dropped and on average 200 tons were dropped every 24 hours. Almost 10,000 people were killed in the onslaught and huge and indiscriminate damage was caused to buildings and utilities. Most of the population was forced to spend the nights in shelters, and the work of the capital was disrupted. On 13th September 1940, Buckingham Palace itself was bombed - an event that quickened feelings of solidarity amongst all classes. "I'm glad we've been bombed" was the Queen's famous remark, "It makes me feel that I can look the East End (of London) in the face". The raids slackened off towards the end of the year, partly because of bad weather conditions, partly because the attack was extended to provincial cities such as Coventry, Manchester, Birmingham, Bristol and Plymouth. At this point about 43,000 had been killed by bombs.

Throughout the autumn of 1940 and with each subsequent Blitz, up to a thousand fires a night were started in any major town during the hours of darkness. Liverpool, Hull, Portsmouth, Glasgow, Plymouth, Manchester, Birmingham, Coventry, Exeter, Leeds, London and all the important ports were badly blitzed. Any unfortunate village near an aerodrome, power station or arms town might be hit, while the enemy emptied surplus bombs over farms, seaside towns or fishing boats in 'tip and run' raids on their return journey. Conflagrations were common, especially when docks and warehouses were shelled and boiling paint, cheese or oil would explode over neighbouring houses in a spreading mass of flames, Firemen slumped on their hoses for hours on end watching red-eyed and helpless as mates were tossed bodily into the air by new blasts. Smoke-choked and exhausted, their efforts were sometimes to no avail.

Civil Defence workers would incur hours of hard physical exertion running from bomb blasts, guiding the homeless, digging for, and finding, parts of bodies among burning debris, often under a spray of water and with crashing walls all around. Women found that the evening work they had volunteered for would stretch into long, distressing hours of night-time labour. In contrast to their peacetime routines, these 'ordinary' women were battered by shock after shock, night after night as they handled the human muddles, which no authority could predict or cater for. A woman ambulance driver records one such night "A warden brought in a basket and said "you're to have these". We asked what it was when he took the paper off and it revealed to be full of all fingers and toes. "The hospital won't take them because it's not a casualty and the mortuary won't because it's not a corpse". Well talk about red tape! The basket was there for two days. Eventually an ambulance driver buried it on the common. In London not a single shop from Oxford Circus to Tottenham Court road was not bombed.

A lull of nearly a year followed. The Luftwaffe was heavily committed on the Eastern Front and therefore had little spare capacity to keep up the attack on Britain. There was an occasional small raid and some sneak attacks by fighter-bombers on eastern and southern small towns. Then on 6th June 1944 'D day' came and our invasion into Europe.

The final phase was experienced by London and the Home Counties only and it took a novel form. Reports of secret long-range weapons being prepared in Germany were dramatically confirmed when pilotless planes carrying high explosives began crashing into the capital on June 15th 1944. By the time the launch sites in France were overrun by Allied troops in late August these V1s or 'flying bombs' had killed 5,475 people, seriously injured 16,000 and caused major blast damage to property. Finally, in early September the unstoppable and even more destructive V2s or 'rocket bombs' succeeded the attackable

V1s. Fortunately, the launch sites of this futuristic weapon were also overrun, but not before 1,724 had been people killed and over 6,000 seriously injured.

What the citizen did not know, and which for obvious reasons he could not be told, was that the bombing would have been a great deal more accurate had it not been for the timely interventions of applied science. The Germans had developed a radio directional beam that could guide their bombers to their targets even at night or in fog. Intelligence Research at the Air Ministry uncovered the potentially devastating secret and scientist quickly came up with a solution in Britain, 'bending' the beam, so that the attackers were directed away from the cities, unknowingly to unload their bombs onto open country. This greatly reduced the effect of the attacks made in the summer of 1940, only one fifth of the bombs falling in the target areas. The Germans, however, then switched to an improved device, known as X-Gerät, which resisted bending or jamming. With this, very accurate raids, such as that on Coventry, were made during the first part of the winter 1940, until British scientists again perfected a way of jamming the device in early in 1941. At the same time there was a breakthrough in designing small radar sets that could be installed in fighter-planes, and improvements were achieved in radio ground-to-air control. During March and April the Luftwaffe's losses were becoming disproportionate to the damage it was causing. There can be no doubt that this aspect, of what Churchill called the 'Wizard War', made a significant contribution to the protection of Britain's cities and people from the worst that the enemy could deliver

Chapter 4
Early Days

Before the war the only semblance of industry in Malmesbury was a Silk Mill situated on the banks of the River Avon at the bottom of the hill on the outskirts of the town.

Wartime photo of Malmesbury Silk mills.

This employed less than one hundred girls but after E.K.Cole Ltd became established at Cowbridge House the mill was requisitioned by the Ministry of Supply and the premises given over to E.K.Cole who used them for storage. The girls who used to work in the Silk Mill were sent to work in the Cowbridge factory.

In the summer of 1939 E.K.Cole Ltd. (Ekco Radio) were approached by the Air Ministry to participate in the development and production of airborne radar equipment. Because of the impending war and the importance of maintaining the utmost secrecy, they were requested to operate in a relatively remote area, where strict security measures could be imposed. It was found impossible to locate ready-made factory premises that fulfilled these conditions and therefore a search was made for a suitable country house capable of the necessary conversion.

Such a property was found on the outskirts of Malmesbury, Wiltshire – Cowbridge House, the residence of a member of the Royal Household, Major Sir Philip Hunloke, G.C.V.O. The house, with numerous outbuildings and fourteen acres of grounds, was purchased for £6,500. Cowbridge House and its outbuildings, albeit somewhat scattered, presented no serious difficulty in the matter of its conversion into factory premises, required for no more than 150 to 200 employees that would be engaged in the operation. The facilities included a machine shop, equipped with power presses and other sheet metal working machinery, various lathes and drilling machines and welding facilities. These were housed in a new building incorporating the "new" stables.

The Secret War Factory

Part of the wartime machine shop

Assembly and testing facilities were located on the ground and first floors of the original house, whilst office facilities were on the upper floors. The old stables, on the banks of the river Avon, which flowed along one side of the property, were converted into a plating and paint spraying shop. All steel parts were cadmium plated and brass parts coppered and silver-plated. Heaven knows how many cyanide and heavy metal salts flowed into that river!

The plating shop at Cowbridge House

A Coil Winding Department producing all the transformers and coils that were required was located in the living quarters, beyond the stable yard, originally used by the gardeners and other outside staff. About twenty of us, who had previous knowledge or experience of radio engineering were drafted to Cowbridge and formed the basis of the production Testing and Test Apparatus Departments. We were the few who "needed to know" what it was all about.

As we were all single men we were housed in a Hostel, Rodbourne House, about three miles away whether we liked it or not! Hostility and suspicion had been directed against the factory from the beginning. It could not be understood why a company from Southend-on-Sea, (wherever that may have been), should buy up a lovely country house and estate; nor could the secrecy around it be explained. The rumour was that it was a place where the sons of wealthy men, who had paid large sums of money to the government, could come to avoid their being conscripted into the armed forces. As a result when we went into the local tobacconist, he had just sold his last packet of cigarettes, and in the pubs they had just pulled the last pint of beer!

Rodborne House – wartime hostel for Ekco workers

Problems, human rather than technical, began almost at the start. The required female workers were at first recruited locally and they had previously worked in domestic service or on farms, and consequently had no industrial background or knowledge of factory life. From the beginning the factory worked a twelve-hour day and this alone came as a shock to them. The working week was from eight am to eight pm, Mondays to Saturdays, with a one-hour lunch break and half an hour tea break. However about a year later finishing time on Friday was seven pm and Saturdays one pm. The Saturday afternoon was particularly welcome as shopping time. The company had little choice in selecting employees, other than technical staff. A requisition was sent to the Ministry of Labour (now the Ministry of Employment) stating their requirements. The machine shop foreman sent by the Ministry was said to be an

Charles Exton

engineer but turned out to be an agricultural engineer greatly, experience in wielding a hammer! with no previous factory experience, or knowledge of production machinery. This man, in charge of fifty or so inexperienced girls, became an industrial relations tinderbox.

At first assembly operators were trained in-house and taught the skills of soldering and assembly operations, but after early 1940 the Ministry of Labour arranged training schools at which all prospective, actually conscripted, employees were assessed and trained before joining the factory work force.

Security was tight, both at the entrance gate and within the factory. There was no wandering about between departments. We few "in the know", subjected to the Official Secrets Act, were classed as "instrument makers" and our identity passes differed slightly from the others and this gave us access to all parts of the factory. The rest of the employees had no idea of what was being produced at the factory and no questions on the subject were encouraged or answered. Some, of course, guessed that there was a connection with radio equipment. Considerable care was taken to disguise the change from a country house to a war time factory and to help with this effort a reconnaissance aircraft regularly flew over the site to check that there were no tell tale signs of activity. Any packing cases etc. left outside had to be covered immediately with camouflage netting. Everything possible was done to maintain the appearance of a country estate.

It was now 1940 when so many massive changes took place and we early 'originals' became almost as bewildered as the hundreds of newcomers. The plans of a factory for not more than two hundred employees had gone completely

The Secret War Factory

The uses of radar multiplied beyond all expectations and over the next two years the enormous rate of expansion at the factory was difficult to manage. Further buildings were added and frequently occupied before completion. The most contentious of these was a large assembly room that could house up to 600 workers. This was built on the lawn in front of the old house and was of reinforced concrete construction with the floor six feet below ground level and was considered "bombproof". It was totally illuminated by fluorescent lighting, as there was no natural light because only very small windows were fitted high up in the walls. This building became hated by all.

A Tool Room, Model Shop, Production Planning and other departments were added to make the factory completely self supporting without the need for any sub-contracting.

It was now found that there was insufficient accommodation within a five-mile radius of the factory and so this area was extended to a twenty-mile radius. About fifteen buses daily ferried up to 500 workers from towns like Chippenham, Cirencester and Swindon and the villages in between. This was really hard in winter as many had to catch buses before seven in the morning and did not reach home again until after nine at night. The only compensation being that those travelling by bus did not have to work overtime. Overtime was not a daily occurrence, but frequent enough when delivery became more urgent than urgent, because everything was urgent! Overtime was from eight until ten in the evening, making it a fourteen-hour day and Sunday mornings were also included.

The National Services Act (No.2) that came into operation on 18th December 1941 affected unmarried women between the ages of 20 and 30. Subsequent legislation extended the age limit until, by 1943, unmarried women under 50 were being called up. "Mobile" women were identified, that is, women who could, according the Ministry of Labour, be shifted about the country without too much domestic disruption, in order to meet labour shortages where they arose. Several hundred of these women were drafted to Malmesbury. E.K.Cole took over five large country houses and converted them into flats and hostels for some two hundred people, which relieved some of the accommodation problems in the town.

The proportion of imported employees to original inhabitants, over a five-mile radius of the factory had risen to over 35%. It is no wonder that the management of the factory had such problems in maintaining production and morale with such a disgruntled and disinterested workforce.

Going Home - Saturday Lunchtime

Some bus drivers brought children in to meet their parents and ride back home with them – photo from the D Grainger collection

Charles Exton

Cowbridge House wartime - The Front Door Entrance

Chapter 5
The Factory, First Impressions

The factory's rapid growth had taken place in the midst of a rural community that was fast disintegrating under the impact of new and ever changing conditions. This same atmosphere of instability and bewilderment was as characteristic of the factory as it was of the town. Very few indeed of the workers (or indeed of the staff) have had any real experience of industrial life. Most of the unskilled female workers were country girls, recruited either from the town itself, or from outlying villages and factory life was something quite new to them. For this reason, the following chapters must not be regarded as describing a typical *industrial* life at all, for there were none of the traditions and background with which the true industrial worker was surrounded. Rather, it was a study of rural adaptation (and failure of adaptation) to a new and startling industrial situation suddenly forced upon them. For the factory has no roots in the place: it has no history of natural growth and development. It was simply dropped there, like a bomb; and just as in the case of a bomb, everyone concerned had to adapt themselves to the situation as best they could.

Charles Exton

The actual site of the factory was in what was, two years ago, a large country house, set in lovely grounds about two miles outside the town. In spite of machinery, the camouflage netting, and the mess of new buildings, something of the house's original charm remains. Here and there amid the ordinary drabness and ugliness of a factory interior were sudden flashes from the past; a lovely polished oak staircase leads up to the offices; occasionally old beams and latticed windows strike a pleasantly incongruous note. Outside, although most of the grounds have been scarred and spoilt by new buildings, both completed and in the process of construction, there were still some pleasant features left. A curving drive arched over with trees forms the entrance, and just in front of the main building was a stretch of water surrounded by shrubs and bushes, and still inhabited by a family of ducks.

The first impressions of the newcomer were therefore not unpleasant. In addition to the fact that the surroundings were really less forbidding than most people expected when they learnt they were to work in a large factory, the authorities really did seem to take considerable trouble to make a new employee arriving from a distance feel welcome. They were taken in the car to a billet (lodgings) that has already been found for them, and then taken up to the factory for her interview and formal application.

The employment office was at the top of a flight of stone steps. It was light and cheerful, with a number of latticed windows, and a low ceiling; probably it was a spare bedroom in the old days. It contained two long deal tables, a desk, and a number of shelves. Four girls were working there, two of them at typewriters. This office served as an ante-room to the labour Manager's own office, which was separated from it by a wooden partition containing a large pane of glass, through which he could see everything going on in the outer office. The Labour Manager himself was constantly going in and out, but this did not stop the chatter and gossip among the office girls at all. They seemed to be on good terms with him, and there is no 'S-sh Here he comes!' about it. Most of the new girls seemed to have found this interview a much less formidable affair than they had expected, and were rather pleasantly surprised by it. Of the Labour Manager, they said in surprised tones "Wasn't he nice!" and almost their only complaint was about the number of forms they had to fill in. "I thought I'd never get to the end of it! As soon as I'd written in one, they'd give me another", or "I was in there for an hour, all that palaver with registrations", and "they ask you every bloody thing, bar what lipstick do you use".

But the horror of these forms was very much mitigated by the friendly and informal attitude that the office girls adopted. There was none of the brusqueness and preoccupied haste, which was so characteristic of labour Exchange girls. On the contrary, they were as helpful and sympathetic as they could be, helping over the difficult parts and reassuring about the doubtful and unanswerable ones.

Conditions of Employment

There were three categories of employees at the Malmesbury Factory. Firstly there were the hourly paid employees who were in the majority and were mostly the production workers. Secondly the weekly paid employees comprising all the office staff and clerks employed in production areas. Finally the monthly paid employees, the departmental managers and foremen and forewomen.

There were marked differences between these categories and it was not just a question of status. Hourly paid employees had to clock in when arriving at 8.00am and again after lunch and at the end of the day when leaving. There were penalties for lateness, a window of three minutes was allowed at eight am. Clocking in, at even four minutes past eight, meant a deduction of a quarter of an hours pay; eight fifteen until eight thirty, half an hour's pay was lost and so on. Overtime working was paid at time and a half during the week and Sunday working was paid at double time. The clock card was used to compile their wages.

Weekly paid staff also had to clock in but at 8-30am and again after lunch but they did not have to clock out when leaving. There was no financial loss for lateness, but there was no additional payment for working overtime. In fact the office staff were rarely called upon to work overtime. However, clerical workers working in the production departments worked the same hours as their department and many elected to be paid hourly. In the beginning, members of the Test Department and other technicians were weekly, paid but when overtime working became quite regular there was quite a revolution so they all transferred to hourly paid staff. The loss of overtime payment outweighed the small advantage of being weekly paid. Monthly staff were not paid overtime either, they did not have to clock in or out, but just signed the attendance book on arrival each morning.

Moreover, hourly paid workers received no pay when they were away from work due to sickness or for any other reason. Weekly paid workers received one week's sick pay during the first year of employment and this increased by increments of one week for each year of service up to a maximum of four weeks sick pay in any one year. The treatment of monthly paid staff was similar, except their maximum payment was for a period of six weeks.

Annual holiday for hourly paid workers was four days, for weekly paid workers it was seven days and two weeks for monthly paid employees. However, these arrangements proved to be academic because after the capitulation of France in June 1940 there were no more Bank Holidays and annual holidays were reduced to four days for everybody. Of course some people managed to wangle a couple of days extra. However getting leave was not easy, as I found out. My fiancée died in hospital up in the Midlands and I applied for compassionate leave to go there and was granted two days. Not enough time to even go to the funeral.

The other main difference affecting the different groups was the canteen. The main canteen was open to all and used by hourly and weekly paid staff although the weekly paid staff did not mix with the hourly paid staff. The monthly paid staff had their own canteen with waitress service who noted down who had what and on each day. On Friday lunchtime everyone was presented with a bill for his week's food and drink which had to be paid on the spot. The menu in the Staff canteen was the same as that in the main canteen. Visitors from the Services and Ministries were entertained in the monthly staff canteen. There was also an Executive Dining Room. This was used by the General Manager and the Assistant General Manager, the Chief Accountant, the Welfare Manager, and Major H. He was an ex Guards Officer and was responsible for security, transport, all maintenance work, all buildings and building work, the vegetable garden etc. he was also the Captain of the Home Guard Unit.

VIP visitors were entertained in the Executive Dining Room. This was the only room where alcoholic drinks were served.

CHAPTER 6
The Effects upon the Local Population

In a tiny country town of ancient cottages and winding streets, with traditions going back to Saxon times, there had suddenly sprung up in a matter of months, a modern war factory employing nearly 1,000 people staffed mainly by brisk, town bred men and women who have no connection with the locality.

If this shock was not enough by itself, it came almost simultaneously with the wartime invasion of evacuees, Ministry officials, soldiers, etc. etc. that has been the lot of most country towns. No wonder that the local population had barely yet woken from the state of dazed bewilderment into which it was stunned by the avalanche of events. Their peaceful old-world town had gone; and in its place is something resembling a London railway terminus, with endless comings and goings of strangers from all parts of the country; with its atmosphere of irritable bustle, impersonal pushing and hurrying.

But this invasion of strangers was not only bewildering. It was also annoying, and highly inconvenient. In peacetime the overcrowding of local buses and shops, the impossibility of getting into the cinema on Saturday afternoons, would probably have been forgiven for the sake of the extra money brought into the town. But now there is no such consolation. Shopkeepers no longer had any desire to attract new customers; a new customer was a nuisance rather than an asset – an unwanted drain on his dwindling supplies. While housewives might be pleased enough to accommodate holiday makers at a high price, it was a different matter to have the house crowded and all the extra housework for 25/- (£1.25) a week, out of which two good meals and all lighting, heating, home, had to be provided. To the ordinary country housewife, who read the paper rarely and only had the vaguest ideas about what is going on outside her own town, these people come not as an essential and inevitable part of the common war effort, but quite meaninglessly out of the blue; like a swarm of locusts they came without warning and without reasons, to eat up already dwindling food supplies; to buy up all the favourite brands of soap and patent medicines; to consume all the fish in the fish and chip shop, leaving her only chips; to cram the local cinema at weekends so that she and her husband can't get near it.

To crown it all, these newcomers usually came in a bad temper. Only a small number of them came here because they *wanted* to; the majority disliked the idea of coming, and were prepared to dislike anything and everything about the place; they were continually comparing it unfavourably with their own homes. Here is a typical conversation between two newly arrived C-class men from Bristol (it did not take place in the hearing of their landlady, but she could not mistake their general mood): "My God, what a dump! Oh my *God* what a dump!"

> "Do you think you'll have to stay long?"
> "God knows, When they send you somewhere quite bloody they usually try to keep you there.
> "I wonder what the pubs are like?"
> "I don't wonder, I can guess. Beer watered down so it tastes like dishwater, and all sold out by eight o'clock"
> "Hm. What the devil will we do in the evenings?

"Go to bed, I suppose .Mrs Whats-it here will ration the light to us, or something, so we can't read. They're always out to do you down in these places".
"I don't think I shall be here more than a few weeks. I think I shall be able to get my release after that".
"Wish I could. When I came for my interview I tried to make myself as dumb as was humanly possible without being certified, but it wasn't any good. I got a letter telling me to come on Monday morning. I got there at two o'clock instead of in the morning, and that night they put me in a place the next best thing to a workhouse. I didn't sleep in the bed at all; I had to sit up in a chair. I couldn't put my head on that pillow. So this morning I went in and told them they could either find me another billet, or they could pay my bill at a hotel, or I would take the first bus back home. The result is this! *This* is where I'm to live, apparently – or rather exist".
"Oh well, I suppose I'll go out and get pickled."

This sort of superficial attitude and grumbling infuriated the locals. They took it as an insult to themselves and their town, an exhibition of snobbishness and superiority. And part of it is; but a much greater part is merely the expression of a bewilderment and sense of upheaval quite as great as the local people's own. Not realising this, and not realising either that these people have been *forced* to come here by an outside authority. The locals, however, took a very firm line about this grumbling. Again and again one heard remarks like this: -

"If she don't like it here, why don't she go back where she came from? *We* wouldn't miss her."
"If we're not good enough for him, then let him take himself off and fine somewhere where he *is* satisfied."

> "They just come down here to get work, and then when they've got it it's just grumble, grumble all the time. If they don't like it, then what do they come for? That's what I always say."

This kind of hostility was directed more against the factory and its employees than against the other newcomers, because the factory was the least understood activity in a place like this. Soldiers were accepted; everyone realised that soldiers are dumped down suddenly in strange places and for no apparent reason. The Air Ministry, too, because of its title, was allowed to have an unquestionable importance. But the factory was a mere excrescence. While it might have been welcomed before the war as providing new opportunities for employment, there was no advantage in this now, for everyone who wanted to be, was already fully employed. Its importance to the war was only vaguely realised, though in view of the low level of war interest, it was doubtful whether it would have made much difference to their attitude if they did realise the reasons for its existence (particularly for its existence here) It was a puzzle to most, and the secrecy surrounding it gave the feeling that there was something to hide. As a result most were very ready to dislike its employees. To start with, there was the feeling that one always gets in a non-industrial area that factory girls are "not nice"; that it is a low sort of occupation

Some of them, too, regard it as a soft sort of job, and there was a lot of talk about men going there to dodge the army

> "They ought to be shot, some of those fellows up there. They've got nothing to do, and they're just sitting tight there because they're frightened they'll have to join the army."

> "There's a lot of men jumped in there at the beginning of the war hoping to be reserved. I'd like to see a good comb-out up there, to catch out those sort of people."
>
> "There isn't anything that a woman couldn't do just as well. It makes me sick to see these great lumps of men hiding away up there while our boys do the fighting. The cowardly swine!"

There was a lot of gossip along these line, the members of staff are included in this.

> "They've got a nice job for themselves, those two (members of staff). Mrs H is supposed to be working in the factory, but *I've* seen her wandering about the streets at eleven in the morning. She's the dodger type; I wouldn't trust that woman further than I could throw a bull by the tail. (Actually Mrs H was the Factory Billeting Officer) And That Mr G. (the Factory Labour Manager) why isn't he in the army? Anyway he's no good for a job like that. He's got a very uneducated voice. You'd have expected a man of culture in his position."
>
> *(Mr G. was a University Graduate with a North Country dialect).*

Underlying all these incidental bickerings and jealousies was the basic distrust of the countryman for strangers from the town. And in this case they were not isolated innocuous strangers, anxious to win the goodwill of the local people and find a place for themselves in the social life of the community. They were unwilling and disgruntled strangers, anxious only to get out of the place as soon as they know how, and go back to their own communities. Such strangers jarred on people who had their town to themselves for a thousand years.

Chapter 7
Life in the Machine Shop

However life in the machine shop was not easy. It was in an extension to what was formerly part of the stables, In spite of the clocking-in cards at the entrance and the hum of machinery within, it still gave much more the impression of a stable than a factory, with its rough walls, high windows and dark cobwebby corners. The main part of the room was occupied by half a dozen or so benches on which were mounted a number of small machines of various kinds. At the back were larger machines standing by themselves and all around the walls were entrances into store rooms, rooms for special electrical work and so on. Altogether about a hundred women and a score or so of men worked there.

At 8am the factory buzzer sounded and a wild scramble started at the entrance of the machine shop (an ordinary wooden small door, such as might lead into any private room). The night workers were trying to clock out exactly at the same moment as the day workers were clocking in, only one person can clock in or out at any one time, and as there is no system of queuing, or order of any kind, it was a case of all-against-all, in which the strongest or heaviest won. Everyone was in a hurry – The day workers because only three minutes grace is allowed for clocking in after the buzzer goes, (later than that and a quarter of an hours pay is stopped). The night workers simply because this is the moment they have been awaiting for the last twelve hours or so. The scrimmage, though ruthless, is fairly good-humoured, and a good deal of joking went on among the groans and exclamations. Through it all the voice of the doorkeeper could be heard occasionally, appealing plaintively to the night workers;" let the young ladies clock in; stand back please and let the day workers clock in".

After getting through this, there was a secondary scramble in the cloakroom, which was small for the number of people using it. The congestion would be even worse were it not for the fact that a number of girls hung about at the benches with their coats and scarves on, waiting for the crush to subside before they went in. There was no sense of hurry in the cloakroom at this hour (there are no definite penalties attached to being late on the bench, once one has actually clocked into the building), and a lot of people took a quarter of an hour or more changing from coats into overalls; and a great deal of talk and chatter went on. At quarter-past eight there were still only about half the girls actually working at their machines (the official time for starting work is at eight o'clock when the buzzer goes). Not until half-past was there anything approaching the whole lot working.

There was a marked tendency every morning for the older women to start work sooner than the young ones. The half dozen or so women over forty who work in this shop were almost always at their machines before five past eight – a time when few of the other machines are in action.

There were various types of machines in the shop – drilling, tapping, etc., each of them operated by one girl, sitting down. On almost all of them the work was very simple placing the part in position (it was usually impossible to do this wrongly) and then the raising or lowering of a handle, or some such action. Usually one could work at one's own speed, letting the finished parts pile up on the bench or in a cardboard box, until someone came and took them away; there was little feeling of hurry or having one's pace dictated by the machine itself, as in a continuous conveyor belt system. With very few exceptions, the work involved neither mental or physical effort of any kind. It was, in fact, just the type of work one heard educated people at war work exhibitions speak of with horror: "I'd go crazy, doing that all day". "The monotony would kill me" and so on. One new employee put it "I was particularly interested to find out what it *does* feel like to be employed thus for hours at a stretch. To my surprise", I found that the boredom is far less than people imagine. In fact, for at any rate the first couple of hours, the work, is definitely pleasant, rather like knitting in a fairly plain pattern. After the rush and scramble of getting up and coming to work through the sleet of a February morning, hurrying to get here on time, fighting to clock in at the door, it is restful and pleasant to sit down in a warm room, with nothing to do but fiddle with bits of metal, and to know that for twelve hours one will not have to think or worry about anything at all".

The feeling was naturally stronger in a newcomer, but undoubtedly throughout the room there was an atmosphere of greater concentration on the job during the first hours of the morning than at any other time of the day. The amount of talking and idling is small, and there was little "clock watching" which formed one of the main features of the latter half of the day.

The first break was at ten o'clock, for ten minutes. About half of the people went up to the canteen for cheese rolls and cups of tea, the rest stayed around the shop, knitting, eating sandwiches and talking. After that the work continued until dinnertime at one o'clock. It was normally a little before eleven that the first signs of slacking off began to appear. People began going to the cloakroom and hanging about for long periods, doing their hair, talking, eating cakes and sandwiches they had brought for dinner and tea. The subject of what time it is (which by four in the afternoon becomes almost an obsession) began to appear in the conversations.

The official time for dinner was one o'clock, and the official time for getting ready for it was five minutes to; actually preparations began a long while before that. Between half past twelve and five to one the cloakrooms were locked (the idea of this was to prevent people getting ready before the appointed time), but what occurred as a result of this is that from twelve-twenty a crowd of girls was to be found in the cloakroom washing their hands, preparatory to going back to the bench and doing nothing whatever for half an hour, so as not to get their hands dirty again before dinner. Another dodge for getting ready before time was the bucket of water in the welding room. It was filled from the water hose there, and the girls, who worked in that part of the room, and their friends, always washed their hands there before time.

The locking of the cloakroom door was the responsibility was of Ginger who was the AEU (Amalgamated Engineer's Union) Shop Stewart. In doing this the Management tried to give the impression that locking the cloakroom door was with the workers cognisance whereas it was, in fact, a management imposition. One day Ginger locked the door, and for some reason, left the machine shop. Five to one came and the door was still locked. The girls had gathered round the door shouting "Where is Ginger" and "Come on Ginger" later this turned to "Ginger, I'll kill you". At two minutes to one Ginger appeared and hearing the remarks of the crowd at the door, threw the key at the girls, turned, and ran!

The Secret War Factory

The real reason for all this ingenuity being expended on circumventing an apparently reasonable rule was that there were only three basins in the cloakroom and it was quite impossible for everyone to wash their black and oily hands in the five minutes allowed for it. (Note: - The Ministry of Labour required standard was one washbasin per twenty-five employees). If the rules were kept, it would mean a lot of people would not get up to the canteen before a quarter past one or later; and the loss of even *one* minute of any of the breaks was regarded as a tragedy. The anxiety not to miss a single second was always marked at dinnertime. At a minute before one, people stood by the door poised as athletes for a race, waiting to rush at the first note of the buzzer. A certain amount of this anxiety was because being late meant being at the end of the queue in the canteen; but it certainly was not all due to this, because people who brought their own sandwiches, and were therefore not concerned with the queue, were equally keen to be in front of the rush!

The dinner hours' were spent by most people in the canteen, knitting, sewing and occasionally reading. If it was fine, quite a number went for strolls in the grounds, or outside up and down the road. Work started again at two o'clock. There was not the same clocking in rush, however, as a lot of people drifted in singly, clocking in early, and went on with their knitting or whatever it was, in little groups by the benches.

It was this stretch of time from two o'clock till six (when there was a half-hour break for tea) that nearly every one dreaded. There was often quite a lot of talk about it among the girls at the end of the dinner hour. Certainly the time from two o'clock till six seemed to go slowly. At about three o'clock one got the feeling that the time would *never* pass; you think to yourself, after a whole hour, it will still only be four o'clock and then two more hours after that. A bewildering sense of helplessness comes over one; nothing one does *can* ever make time pass as long as that.

One gets the feeling that time isn't passing on its own at all; that one has to drag the clock hand round the minutes by willpower. One begins to make idiotic bargains with oneself like, if I drill a hundred of these holes without looking up, then by that the time I do look up ten minutes will have passed.

Between three and five in the afternoon more slacking and idling went on than one would have thought possible in a war time factory. Sometimes one could look along the bench and see not more than one girl in four actually working. But the others were rarely doing anything that could be definitely picked on by the foreman, such as knitting or reading. For example one would be sitting with her hand on the handle of the machine, as if to pull it down, and yet somehow not doing it; another would be patting her hair; another just settling down after a visit to the cloakroom, and so on.

It was at this hour that the activities known to the authorities as "lavatory mongering" were at their height. People drifted out to the cloakroom, and remained there for half an hour or more, eating sandwiches, talking, reading and often doing nothing at all. This in spite of the fact that the cloakroom was most uninviting, containing simply three wash basins, two lavatories, and a few square feet of stone floor. There were no chairs or benches to sit on, not even a ledge on which to lay a bag or comb. Anything was welcome as long as it was a change from sitting at the bench.

Now and then sporadic bursts of singing started in some part of the room or other and continue for a few minutes. It was usually a purely local affair, confined to the occupants of a few square yards of a bench – nothing approaching community singing throughout the room ever developed. Singing seemed to be a symptom of boredom more than exuberance, as it occurred mostly during the dead period of ordinary weekday afternoons

The Secret War Factory

(three to five), and only rarely on Saturdays, or at the end of a spell of work.

After five o'clock there was a marked recovery in both cheerfulness and concentration on the job. The feeling that a break (tea at six o'clock) was in sight had a definitely stimulating effect. One felt that the worst was over, because the time after tea, from half past six seemed to fly at an extraordinary speed. Everyone felt this; it is remarked on spontaneously by a variety of girls. On the first day at tea, a girl said consolingly to a newcomer "You'll be alright now, the time goes ever so quick after tea". "That's right," said her friend "It goes lovely after tea, Funny isn't it? It never drags, not after teatime. It was quite true, we found, and it never failed. Sometimes after a particularly long afternoon one used to feel sure that *this* time it would go slowly after tea too. But somehow it never did. Eight o'clock always arrived as something as a surprise, just as one was feeling (for the first time since ten in the morning) that one wouldn't mind going on for another hour or so.

For clocking out in the evening there was normally some attempt at a queue, instead of a mere scramble. People lined up around the room in something approaching the order in which they were ready, though the ruling was very loose, and some used to try and slip in near the front without raising much protest.

It is clear from the preceding sections that in the Machine Shop as a whole there was little interest in the work. The main preoccupation seemed to be how to make the time between the breaks pass as quickly as possible, and to wait for the evening to come. "Roll on, eight o'clock" was a phrase heard over and over again during the course of the day, in all parts of the room. Some of the girls were very conscious of this preoccupation of theirs, and often one heard quite long conversations on the subject of how quickly or how slowly the time was going on a given day and it is curious that there was always unanimous agreement about whether a given stretch of time has gone quickly or slowly.

To some extent this intense interest in the passing of time serves as a substitute for interest in the work, but it had a curious psychological effect. At the end of the day one tended to feel not tired, but as if one had not had a day at all – missed it out somehow- coming out into the blackout one got a sort of angry shock of surprise to find that it was night again already, when it seems that it ought to be fairly soon after breakfast, so little has happened in the interval. Somehow the same things happened on a larger scale as the weeks went by. But this attitude of passive waiting for the day to be over did not imply merely lack of interest in the actual jobs to be done. It implied also a profound and very significant reluctance to accept the twelve hours spent in the factory as part of real life at all; it was simply a blank patch between one brief evening and the next. It also meant that it was extremely difficult to rouse *any* kind of corporate attitude to anything, whether it be social activities, criticisms and complaints, political activity or anything else. This apathy about the factory and everything to do with it was about the biggest problem, with which the authorities were faced, and it laid at the bottom of most of the problems.

To some extent this was of course, inevitable, as much of the apparatus made was of a highly secret, as well as of a considerable technical nature. But not only did most of the machine shop girls not understand what they are making, but also most of them had not the faintest desire to understand. Only on very rare occasions, and from particular types of girl, was any spontaneous reference to what a given part might be used for, even from the most limited point of view. It is interesting that older women usually had a much clearer idea of what they are doing than the younger ones in this sort of way. Interest in the way machines work was also rare, and when it did appear it is generally in the older women.

It was felt by the management that one of the big problems of this type of factory was that the work seemed superficially to be remote from the war; that it was not of obvious immediate use, like making bullets and shells. They felt that lack of interest in the work was largely due to this – that the girls did not feel they were contributing to the war. A good deal of trouble was taken to emphasise and publicise the importance of the work for the war effort, but this was difficult as the end product from the factory and its use was a top secret that could never be revealed.

Factory pep talk explaining the importance of piece parts. – photo from the Sykes-Lipman collection

As far as the machine shop was concerned however, evidence showed some of this anxiety was misdirected. The trouble was not that the girls did not realise that their work was important to the war, *but the majority of them were so little interested in the*

Charles Exton

war that they did not care whether their work was important to it or not. As in so many country places, to the women at least, the war was simply a thing that happens, like thunderstorms, or an earthquake, and victory was similarly a thing that would happen. All that could be done was to hope that it would happen soon, as one hopes for fine weather. The idea that anything one did or did not do could possibly have any bearing on it all came very slowly. This negative attitude to the war was to a large extent marked among factory workers like these than among the rest of the population in the area. For, paradoxical as it seemed, life in a twelve-hours-a-day war factory made one feel further from the war than one could in any other type of life.

It is hard for anyone who has not tried it, to realise the curious, almost exhilarating sense of the slipping away of all responsibilities that came over people after a few days in this sort of work. From eight in the morning till eight at night, life was taken off one's hands, completely and absolutely. All personal and social claims and responsibility vanished; and, in these lower grades of work, no alternative responsibility for the work emerged, it did not stop here. When a girl got home at half-past eight or nine at night, what awaited her? Someone else had, of necessity, coped with the rationing and shopping problems; someone else had tidied the house, planned tomorrow's meals, and done the washing. Someone else had seen that the rent and milk bill has been paid; someone else had probably written any letters that needed to be written.

All that the average girl had to cope with when she got home (because this was about all she physically had time to cope with) was getting undressed and putting curlers in her hair. It was not surprising that, after a few weeks of this sort of life, a girl began to feel isolated from the outside world, and lose her sense of responsibility towards it. By the nature of her work and its long hours, she was cut off from daily life of her community;

The Secret War Factory

she was sheltered from its day-to-day difficulties and problems (i.e. Rationing. transport, etc.).

The attitude she inevitably developed to life as a whole coloured even more markedly her attitude to the war. It became evident that the average working-class woman's interest in the war was kept alive not so much by large scale tragedies, like the loss of another piece of territory, but by the personal inconveniences; rationing, blackout, shortages and so on.

This, then, was probably the main reason for the almost complete lack of war feeling that characterised the machine shop. Never once, from any of the girls, was there any suggestion that we ought to do this or that because of the war; never was there any shadow of public opinion directed against slacking or dodging of any kind. Expert dodgers were merely envied for their ability to get away with it.

Anything which interrupted work, even for a few moments was acclaimed with unrestrained delight. One morning the electricity which drove the machines kept on suddenly going off for a few minutes; and every time this happened a spontaneous shout of "Hurray!" went up all over the room; and corresponding groans as soon as it started again. Never was there any suggestion that it mattered that time was being wasted and production held up. And another morning, when for two hours the electricity didn't go on at all, the only complaint was from those working hand presses and other non-electrical processes. They complained it wasn't fair that they should have to work while others didn't!

While the situation remained like this, appeals to patriotism as an incentive to increased production were almost valueless. The patriotic posters ("It all depends on me". "We want your help" etc. etc.") that plastered the walls of every room in the factory were so much ornamental scrollwork for all the notice that was taken of them, by the machine shop at least.

The main reason for the lack of corporate feeling at work was just one of the symptoms of the general reluctance to put any heart or interest into any aspect of the factory life.

A particular problem we had in the machine shop was 'ownership' since with few exceptions nobody's work depended on anybody else's work. In most cases the work was brought from the store room, given to a girl to do, and then taken away again; there were only a few occasions where the part was handed from one girl to another, each performing a different operation on them. Occasionally it happened that a part had to go through two or perhaps three machine shop hands before it disappeared but this was not enough to create the spirit of corporate achievement which was possible in other parts of the factory, where the same parts had to pass down an entire bench, each girl adding to or altering in some way.

Some of the girls were very conscious of their position in the machine shop. They felt that they were looked down on by the rest of the factory – which to some extent was true, but not nearly as much as some of them imagined. The machine shop girls tended to exaggerate the extent of this feeling, and many of them were very much on the defensive about it. Others reacted to the feeling in another way, by belittling the machine shop themselves, and prided themselves on "not mixing" with the others. Complaints actually voiced about specific subjects were exceedingly few, the whole attitude to the factory was too casual to breed anything but vague, undirected moaning and dislike. Such complaints as there were can be classified as follows: -

The Secret War Factory

(a) *Being here at all.*
Talk about the possible ways and means of getting out was frequent, but few got so far as to take any practical steps to secure their release. A lot of people regretted bitterly that they ever let themselves be put here: "I wish I'd volunteered for the A.T.S. when I could have done. You get more freedom there". "I'd never have come here, but I never knew they'd make me stop like this, I only wanted to be here for a bit to be near my mum".

Perhaps one of the most vivid pictures in the minds of most of the machine shop girls was the vision of the Last Day in the factory. Often it crept into the talk, and sometimes one heard conversation like this, between two girls in their early twenties, both conscripts: "The day the war is over I'll be the first one out of here. I'll be down that path and out before they've finished announcing it".

Although dislike of being in the factory at all was by far the most often voiced complaint, it was not exactly a grievance. The girl's did not feel that they *ought* not to be made to stay; they do not think of it in those terms at all. It was simply a thing that happened to them, and they disliked it, and so they complained just as they might complain about the weather. There was only rarely any suggestion that someone ought to do something about it.

(b) *Long Hours*
Almost everyone felt that the hours were too long, but there again there was not much coherent idea that anything could or should be done about it. Objection to them was expressed simply by vague moaning, or by taking time off whenever and wherever possible. Complaints were focused on lack of leisure rather than tiredness.

(c) *Break Periods*
Here and there among the aimless gloom about the four-hour stretch from two till six in the afternoon, were occasional demands for a break during this period. "It would make all the difference, wouldn't it, if we had ten minutes to look forward to at half-past three.

(d) *Cloakroom*
Complaints about the cloakroom were a frequent grievance. In point of fact, the cloakroom was far too small, but complaints heard were not usually about this as so much as about minor irregular shortcomings like lack of soap, no hot water, wet and dirty towels.

There was a general apathy of the girls about their whole life in the factory but though these complaints were heard frequently, there were never any strong suggestions of trying to get the authorities to do something about it. Even in the case where the bolt that had come off one of the lavatory doors, nobody seriously considered asking to have it replaced (which certainly would have been done). It was simply grumbled about and left at that.

The charge-hands in the machine shop were all men, in their twenties and early thirties. Each of them paid much more attention to the mechanical side of their job – setting up and generally looking after the apparatus and machinery – than to their other task of discipline and leadership among the girls on the bench. They almost all adopted the same attitude to the girls – one of amused tolerance; nothing a girl could do would bring her a reprimand from a charge-hand; the worst she had to fear is a piece of good-humoured sarcasm.

The girls themselves revelled in this situation. If the charge-hands choose to look on them (with amused masculine superiority) as scatterbrained little nitwits, who can't do anything right, then what could be easier than to accept this role and make it cover for any and every kind of carelessness and laziness? This attitude often took the last shreds of responsibility for their actions from the girl's shoulders, and gave the final touches to that carefree atmosphere which was the machine shops attraction.

Although there was not much respect for the authority of charge-hands – there is no "Look out- he's coming" atmosphere as there was in the case of the foreman – they were all well liked, with one exception. It was interesting that this exception was the only one of the charge-hands who did not adopt the attitude described above; in fact he deliberately tried to avoid it. He said "I don't try to make myself superior, like some of them. I always treat the girls as my equals – I'm not supposed to, but I do. I've come in with the workers. I'm a worker myself and not ashamed of it".

This did not go down well with the girls, who much preferred to be regarded as not responsible for their own actions. The male charge-hands, whatever their effect on production were certainly much more popular than the female charge-hand who used to be there – a lot of girls consciously disliked working under a woman. The foreman in the machine shop was almost universally popular. He managed to combine the same air of tolerant amusement that made the charge-hands popular.

Wartime note from the Works Manager to the machine shop: -
The supervision in this shop has of necessity been recruited from the best elements in the rank and file. Naturally they lack supervisory training and in default thereof the Management are endeavouring to guide promoted supervisory grades in the technique of supervision. The expansion of War Industry has made supervisory grades in all industries the rarest of the rare.

Chapter 8
Machine Shop Difficulties

The real problem department, which caused the management most concern, was the Machine Shop, where output had been declining and this became a major problem. Other departments became affected due to lack of parts from the Machine Shop. The management and the foreman had been changed. There was ample machine capacity and a sufficient, largely female, labour force, but output per man/woman hour was unacceptably low. The majority of the conscripted girls regarded the war with negative emotions as something to be endured, as food and other shortages were endured. The long hours of monotonous, repetitive work requiring the minimum of attention, (let alone involvement), brought morale to its lowest ebb. It should be remembered that the usual forms of industrial discipline could not be applied in those days. This was because the ultimate weapon, i.e. the fear of the sack could not be affected. The Company did not choose the employees; they were supplied by the Ministry of Labour and, unless it could be proven that an employee was totally incompetent, it was almost impossible to have them replaced. Those that were dismissed, other than those who left on medical grounds, were automatically conscripted into the armed forces, and this thought calmed many rebellious souls.

Charles Exton

The only immediate answer to the machine shop problem was to bring in more male employees and start a night shift. The buses bringing in the day shift at eight in the morning took the night shift home, and at eight in the evening brought the night shift in and took the day shift home again. Later the staff of the two shifts were mixed, that is half of the day shift girls went on nights and half of the night shift men went on days, and output went up. The girls seemed to get some emotional stimulus from working nights. It was then decided, in order to economise on male labour, to dispense with the male night shift and expand the number of female workers and split them between day and night, alternating shifts each month. The start of the night shift brought a sigh of relief to the Home Guard, since extra security staff was now on duty at night and the armed guard could be dispensed with.

The questions of low morale, lack of interest and resentment concerned the management deeply. The company made what efforts they could to augment the lack of social amenities. They hired the small local cinema on Sunday evenings and seats could be booked at the factory during the week. Any surplus tickets were given to the army unit garrisoned at the local YMCA, the local council objecting to tickets being sold on a Sunday.

A Social Centre, with Government backing, was also set up in the centre of the town. This contained a small hall for dancing, a bar, reading and games rooms etc. It was well patronised by the "old original" employees but the conscripted workers, for whom it was intended, remained aloof and disinterested and largely ignored the place.

Michael Lipman, the factory manager, in an effort to better understand the issues made an approach to Tom Harrison, Director of Mass-Observation, and wrote, "The winter of 1941/42 saw saturation point reached in personnel, and the

The Secret War Factory

problems of war fatigue, lack of concentration, and general absence of "morale" reached proportions which make it necessary to have some objective survey undertaken". This approach and the identity of the observer, who became an employee, and worked in the machine shop and on the assembly lines, was known to only three people in the entire organisation. Whilst the report was undoubtedly helpful it, of course, could not supply remedies, but imagine the consternation of the management when in 1943 Mass-Observation published the report in form of a book. The last straw was when the local W.H.Smith bookshop displayed a placard saying, "Come and read about your own factory". All at a time when secrecy was still the byword.

Note; - Mass-Observation was an organisation base at Oxford University and investigated and reported upon social issues of the day. For instance, it reported to the Government on the effect of enemy bombing on the people and another report was on the effect of food rationing. The majority of these reports remained confidential to the instigators of the report and it was never known why the report on the Malmesbury factory was published in book form. The book, of course, never revealed the name of the factory or its location. However, to any employee reading the book it was obvious it was about them, since the observer referred to many people by their nicknames and Management could be identified by the use of their initials. Clearly much that was written was not complimentary and many local readers took umbrage. The publication of the book had a detrimental effect as the employees blamed the Management of spying and relations between the two became even more strained.

CHAPTER 9
The Main Assembly Department

In the Main Assembly Department were long, wide benches running the length of the building, beyond which was the Test Department. Each bench was devoted to the assembly of one specific piece of equipment, such as a receiver, indicator or transmitter for example. Girls sat at each side of the bench, which had a large storage shelf running down the centre. Assembly progressed in stages. Starting, at the top end of the bench, with a bare chassis the first assembly stage was completed and it was then passed down to the next girl, who completed her part and then similarly passed it down the line until at the end was a complete unit. Inspectors sat at various places down the line for intermediate inspection stages and a final stage was at the end of the line before passing the completed unit to the Test Department

Charles Exton

Assembly line: Note the lack of natural light

It was the job of the Production Planning Department to break down the assembly operations into stages that would take about the same amount of time to complete and to produce the illustrations and fixtures required to assist each operation. They also had to demonstrate and train, where required, girls who had particularly difficult or intricate operations to perform. It usually took several weeks to get an assembly line running smoothly but most "runs" were quite long, usually 500 or 1,000 units. During the setting up of an assembly line the Test Department would become familiar with the particular piece of equipment and the test and calibration procedures that were required.

Each assembly line also had a female "Charge-Hand", whose job it was to ensure that each girl had a sufficient supply of her particular bits and pieces, so that the progress of the units down the line went smoothly, without any hold up, and through the various inspection stages, so that the daily output target was achieved. In addition she was responsible for discipline on the line. This was mainly to ensure there was a prompt return from the canteen after lunch and tea breaks, that visits to the cloakroom were not too frequent, or too lengthy, and that there was no nibbling of sandwiches or biscuits on the production line. Smoking was only permitted in the Machine Shop.

Each assembly line also had its "Progress Chaser" and his job was to make certain that the line had sufficient supplies for at least that day's output. He might, for example, be rushing to the Coil Winding Department chasing the completion of transformers his line needed, or parts from the Machine Shop or Small Parts Assembly. Essentially he had to be a good salesman to convince the foreman of the particular department concerned that his needs were greater than anyone else's. As no parts could be moved from one location to another without being inspected and tested and accompanied by the essential "Movement Slip", he also had to cajole the appropriate inspector, or tester, to stop what he was doing to complete the work on his parts and write out the required "Movement Slip". All parts going to the Main Assembly Lines had to go via the Main Stores where they were recorded, so there was more paper work to move the goods into Stores and issue them out to the Assembly Line.

This question of inspection and "Movement Slips" served a real purpose. Each Inspector and Tester had his own rubber stamp that contained his identity number. All parts that were large enough had to be individually stamped by the inspector who had passed them as being satisfactory. He would then make out a "Movement Slip" passing the parts to the next production operation, or to Stores, as the case may be. Thus, if there was a failure of a part or sub-assembly was found in the Test Department, or even later in Service, then, from the faulty part itself, or from the paperwork the identity of the inspector or tester originally passing the part was known. If an inspector lost his stamp, a record was made of the date of the loss and the number was withdrawn. The inspector concerned was immediately transferred from the Inspection Department, probably on to a production operation. There was no second chance.

If, on the assembly line, there was a shortage of purchased components, such as resistors or capacitors, the assembly line progress chaser would contact the purchasing progress chaser, who would in turn chase the supplier concerned or, more likely contact one of the "outside" progress chasers. There were a number of these based in various parts of the country, usually located adjacent to the major components suppliers. They would then visit the company concerned to chase up the late delivery and frequently take supplies directly from them and put the urgently required items on passenger train to the nearest main line station to Malmesbury. In extreme cases a dispatch rider or van would be sent to collect the items. Rail transport was almost exclusively used for general deliveries rather then road transport due to the wartime shortage of petrol and diesel fuels.

During wartime there was a shortage of raw materials and components of all kinds. Manufacturers and stockists were only allowed to supply customers whose orders carried Ministry Contract Numbers, each contract number included a priority rating code and the highest priority ratings had to be supplied first. Airborne Radar Contracts had one of the highest priority ratings.

At the end of each assembly line was a large red light, rather like a pedestrian crossing light. When an assembly line was forced to stop production due to a shortage of parts the red light was switched by the charge-hand, usually accompanied by an outbreak of cheering from the operators on that line because this meant a break from work. The red light had other effects, the assembly foreman, the assembly superintendent, and the chief progress chaser all came rushing up to find the reason for the stoppage. The poor line chaser got bawled out for allowing the situation to arise and general panic ensued until supplies were restored and the red light turned off.

How did life on the assembly lines compare with the machine shop? Occasionally girls were transferred to the Assembly Department – apparently as a punishment for excessive idling and wasting time in the Machine Shop. All such girls agreed that to be sent to the assembly lines was in the nature of a tragedy. This seemed at first rather surprising, because the assembly work was considered more interesting, and to be moved there in some sense was a promotion. Some of the reasons for their dislike were that on first impressions the main assembly area was of a vast low roofed hall, out of reach of the daylight and lit eternally by white fluorescent lights. Running lengthways down it were lines of benches, covered with what seem at first sight to be thousands and thousands of coloured toys, like a fantastic Christmas shopping store. A closer look revelled that this effect was being produced by all the many different coloured wires and plugs that were being used.

Even at first glance, one could see that the atmosphere was different from that of the machine shop. Many of the girls were engaged on elaborate and complicated work, demanding a good deal of attention. The slapdash, carefree atmosphere of the machine shop was replaced by one of purposeful attention – sometimes even interest. The type of girl was different too; one girl who had a particularly fiddly and difficult job, demanding fingers both small and strong, for wrestling with tiny but obstinate screws and fittings. She had worked at it for several months now, and was one of the few girls who could manage it. She said of it: "they put me on easy jobs sometimes, but I like something to struggle with. I like going on and on until I've got it right, so when I'm finished I can think to myself – There, I did that! Aren't I a clever girl?"

This sort of attitude – quite unknown in the machine shop – belonged to some degree to many of the girls there. The reason was simple. Instead of completely monotonous, repetitious work, most of the girls worked on jobs that took twenty minutes, or half an hour each, not just a few seconds, and most of them required a fair degree of at least manual skill, and also attention. Another very important factor was that a set number was given for the day. Thus, the whole bench was supposed to turn out, say, twenty completed units a day, which meant that each girl had to perform twenty of her operations. This gave one a totally different attitude to time. There was no longer the blind waiting for the time to pass, but rather a certain amount of directed effort to get a given job done in a given time. Not that there were any special penalties for not getting twenty done, but if one particular girl was being very slow over her part of the work, it meant the next girl, to whom she hands on her work when it is finished, was kept waiting; and the psychological effect of knowing that someone of your own sort was sitting waiting for you to finish (even if you also know that she doesn't mind waiting) provided an automatic, almost unconscious, incentive greater than any reprimand. In fact, so strong was this feeling that most people's ambition was to "have plenty in hand" – that is to say, get ahead of the next girl on the process, so that there was a pile waiting for her to do. This gave the comfortable sense of being able to slack off, without the irritating feeling of someone sitting and waiting for more.

A good deal of talk went on during work in the Assembly. Conversation was much easier than that in the machine shop, because there was a lot less noise and the girls were sitting closer together – only two or three feet between each girl, whereas in the machine shop most of the machines were five or six feet apart.

Complaints and Criticisms

(a) *By Newcomers from the Machine Shop*
From the foregoing description it might be imagined that anyone coming from the machine shop would be thankful for the relief from boredom offered by this more interesting and constructive work. It seems that to most of them this advantage was more than offset by the burden of responsibilities, with which a year or more in the machine shop had ill fitted them to cope. Undoubtedly, after being in the machine shop for even a short time and then coming out again, the girls seemed to miss very much the sense of complete and utter freedom from cares and responsibilities of all kinds; the feeling of security and peace that came from having every moment of the day, whether pleasant or otherwise, planned and arranged for by someone else. Many of the complaints heard from these girls referred to this new and unwelcome responsibility.

The change of times for breaks had also been a big grievance. In the machine shop the breaks were ten minutes at ten am; dinner from one to two, tea from six to six-thirty In the assembly there was no break in the morning; dinner from twelve to one; a short tea break from three-twenty to three-thirty; and then a half-hour break from five-thirty to six. The girls from the machine shop couldn't get over the loss of the ten-minute break in the morning and they disliked coming back from tea at six instead of six-thirty. The two hours until eight seeming much longer than the hour and a half to which they had been accustomed. They forgot that the long four-hour stretch in the afternoon, which they used to dread, had now been broken up. It seems that once psychologically adapted to one set of hours any change feels like a change for the worse.

(b) By Permanent Assembly Workers

The assembly girls were more vocal in their grievances than were the machine shop girls. As in the machine shop, the most frequently and most bitterly discussed grievance was the length of hours. But the assembly girls were much quicker to suggest that they *ought* to be cut down – not merely to wish helplessly. There was, too, a certain amount of thought out criticism of mismanagement, with reference to other factors than mere personal likes and dislikes. A complaint of this sort heard several times was about time sheets; the time sheets were small printed forms, about three inches by two inches, on which each girl had to fill in each day what job she was working on, and what time she started and finished. No one could make out quite what the point of this was, as all the information was already on the clock cards, but whereas in the machine shop no one worried about it one way or the other, in Assembly one heard remarks like this:

"It's wicked the way they waste paper here. The way they make you start a new clocking card, if there's only two entries used on the last one. And the time sheets, that's a waste of paper. They never look at them, I know they don't. They don't use them at all, these office girls. They just collect them up and never look at them. It's a wicked waste." (*Actually the time sheets are an essential part of the costing system*)

A frequent complaint from the girls who had been on assembly for some time was about the room itself. As it was very large and lit all the time by artificial lights. Though the lighting is good from the physiological point of view, many of them felt bitterly about never seeing daylight: "you sometimes think you'll go mad, in summer time, shut up in here like night time, when the sun is shining away outside". Or, "I hate this place. If you could just see a bit of the sky out of the window even, it wouldn't be so bad".

Note: - The original Assembly Department was in part of the old mansion house, but this became too small, so this new building was constructed partially underground and made as bomb proof as possible against possible enemy action.

Those who remembered the old assembly department, looked back on it with longing.

Front of Cowbridge House before the Main Assembly extension was built.

I don't like this new place. We used to be upstairs, it was so nice, like a real old mansion, you went up a lovely old polished staircase, and all the oak walls and everything. I used to look forward to coming in the mornings, it was so pretty. You could have all the windows open, and look out on to the lawn, and there was a fountain and a goldfish pond where this place is built now. We could see all the grass and flowers in the sun, and smell all the lovely fresh air coming in, in the summer. It seemed wicked to knock it all to pieces and put this thing up.

We saw them doing it, and we thought it was wicked. It's all clammy down here, like being in prison, and you never see the sun any more"

"I used to be happy in the Assembly, but I'm browned off now. I don't like being inside like this. I sometimes feel if I don't get out I shall go balmy. Do you know, sometimes, I think to myself, is it morning or afternoon now? You can't tell whether it's summer or winter or day or night. I don't like it

In this long hall of concentrated, skilful war effort there was a sort of everlasting simmer of minor discontent. Whilst the charge-hands in the machine shop were all men, in the Assembly they were all women; this was indeed one of the objections the machine shop girls had to working in the Assembly.

"It's cleaner here I know, but I don't like the charge-hands. They're always watching over you, and they come and tell you off if you're standing around".

The girls actually in the Assembly did not object as much. Women charge-hands were undoubtedly stricter disciplinarians than men, but the assembly girls took a certain amount of discipline for granted, in a way in which the machine shop girls were unwilling to do. The assembly girls, however, though they did not object to discipline as such, were very sensitive to the manner in which it was administered.

Take two of the charge-hands, Mrs B and Mrs C, who were both equally strict as far as things they forbade and allowed were concerned, but their manner of putting it across differed very much, as did their popularity with the girls. Mrs B. was a youngish blonde woman, with a gentle, rather childlike voice, who always looked tired and harassed. She enforced her demands by a sort of unassuming appeal, which seemed much more effective than direct firmness.

The girls liked her, and made efforts to see that nothing they did would get her into trouble.

> "I like our charge-hand. Sometimes I feel I want to kiss her when she's so nice – she speaks to you so politely, and no bullying. There's no "do this" – "do that" about her it's always "please" and "will you".
>
> "She's ever so nice, she never tells you off if you don't finish all your sets, but I like to finish if I can, because she gets the blame in the end if this bench is slower than the rest".

Mrs C. on the other hand, while she enforced the same degree of discipline always seemed to be enforcing a more stringent code, as these remarks show.

> "She's a terror – always hanging around – "Don't do this" – "Don't do that".
> "You always feel you mustn't talk if she's around. Of course she can't stop you talking, not if you're getting on at the same time, but you feel like that. "I don't like her. You feel on the jump when she's around".

Many of the charge-hands failed to realise the immense importance which the girls attached to finding out *who's fault* a given mistake was and it was all too easy for the charge hands to fall foul of this by equally blaming two girls, one of whom had made a mistake.

The following incident illustrates this point. The screws on a certain piece of work were found by Inspection to have been screwed up too tight. This might have been the fault of the girl who originally had to put them in, Mary, or it might be the fault of Rose, who later on had to unscrew them to do her own job, and then screw them up again the way she had found them. When it was found that they arrived in Inspection done up too tight, the charge-hand took the apparently simple course of telling both girls just how tight to do them. But this aroused a storm of protest.

> "They were all right when I sent them up, she must have done it when she tightened them up again".
> "I didn't I did them up the way they came".
> "You couldn't have done. I've been on this job for months, and no one's complained before…"
> "Well, all I know is, I did them up just the way they came to me".
> "I don't care who did it", the charge-hand breaks in, "All I care is it isn't done again. You can fight it out for yourselves whose fault it is".

She could hardly have said anything more tactless. The result was half a morning spent on more and more heated wrangling, until at last the foreman had to intervene and sort the rights and wrongs of the case in all its detail.

These sort of problems were perhaps the most difficult to sort out since clearly unlimited time could not be spent on assessing rights and wrongs, but on the other hand, if the management considered the question of blame quite irrelevant and simply left it in mid-air, the girl who had done nothing wrong and knows it was not her fault was left with a quite disproportionate sense of grievance, which usually lasted for days and even weeks. One of the secrets of Mrs B's popularity was that she always took the trouble to investigate matters of this sort – even if she did not come to any conclusions, she gave the girl the feeling that she was being listened to, which is what she chiefly wanted. This problem was the more worth considering, as it was the girls who took a certain amount of pride and interest who invariably are the most sensitive to implied or imagined slights.

In the Assembly, the foremen were for the most part much less well known, and hardly at all talked about. Mr. B., the foreman in the machine shop, was well known to everyone, and made his personality felt. In the Assembly there are a number of girls who barely knew who their foreman was and apart from the occasional,

"Look out, he's coming!" the foremen were rarely mentioned or talked of. Their authority was recognised in a very impersonal way.

CHAPTER 10
Test and Inspection

All goods entering the factory went through the Goods Inwards Inspection Department. This department grew to about fifty inspectors. Every resistor, capacitor and other purchased component were individually tested for performance or value and tolerance. High voltage components were additionally tested for breakdown voltage under partial vacuum. Everything that could be tested was tested to its specification and the test equipment was extensive and elaborate. Nothing went into stores without being inspected and tested. Goods being moved from one location to another had to be accompanied by a "Movement Slip".

This was made out by the appropriate inspector and recorded the number of items stamped and passed as being acceptable and the number of items rejected. Rejected items and other rubbish were, where possible, burned on site. Rubbish disposed of off site was carefully inspected to ensure that no scrapped items could identify the purpose of the factory. Valves and Cathode Ray Tubes were supplied by the Ministry of Supply, already tested, on "Embodiment Loan" at no cost to the company. All embodiment loan items were stored and recorded separately in a Bonded Store and Ministry of Supply Auditors frequently inspected the stock and the records. Valves and cathode ray tubes were only issued to the Test Department and fitted to equipments as part of the Test procedure.

The ratio of Testers and Inspectors to production workers was high; about 20%. This was to ensure the quality of the work and that parts were correctly assembled and wired so that the equipment would work first time, when received by the test department. With employees inexperienced in this type of work and to reduce wastage, there were many inspection stages during the course of assembly. The Production Planning Department engaged two artists who drew pictures of tag boards of resistors and other assemblies and then coloured them in watercolours so that resistors, for example, were shown in their colour codes.

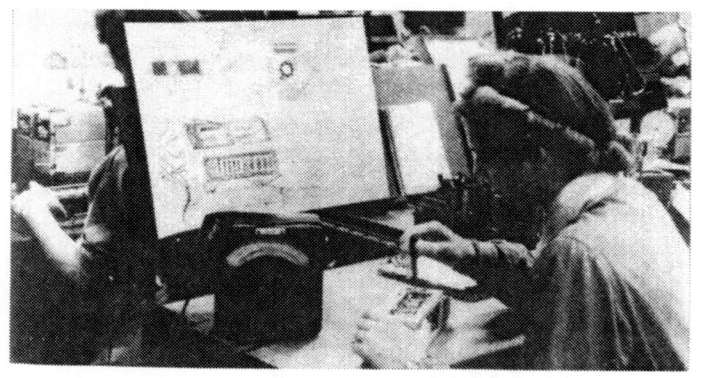

Assembly working using watercolour sketch.

Some drawings were exploded views in order to clarify the sequence of assembly. These were indeed real works of art! Both assemblers and inspectors used these pictorial aids extensively as neither were familiar with, or had any knowledge of electronic bits and pieces.

Outside of the Test Department it is unlikely that anyone could understand a circuit diagram, not that they were ever likely to

The Secret War Factory

get the opportunity to see one! With the increase in production demand and now that extra space and employees were available, the bottleneck became the Test Department. The Ministry had long ago put an embargo on increasing the number of "need to know" personnel, but we were desperately in need of competent technicians to increase the output from the Test Department. The Ministry had the attitude that if we were given competent technicians they would soon be able to work out for themselves the purpose of the equipment and, dear me, that would never do; we must train our own staff who only had a limited technical knowledge. How on earth do you let people with limited knowledge dip their hands into transmitters, modulators and power units which had anything up to 8,000 volts flying about inside.

Another tack was tried. Technical grades in certain RAF and Naval Units were asked to volunteer for civilian work, testing equipment. This was to be for three monthly renewable periods. The initial rush was limited to twenty and they worked very well but disaster struck at the end of the three months. To a man, they said "no more", life in the services being a piece of cake compared to the twelve-hour and longer working day at the factory. There were no more volunteers. The next scheme was to use University students, chiefly those reading physics or engineering, who were given the option of spending their last year of study in an essential industry instead of University. This scheme worked well, particularly as some of the students were female and this brightened up the Test Department no end. Not until the end of their year did they realise that they would not be allowed to leave.

Apart from the Goods Inwards Inspection Department, inspectors were dotted about in various departments at strategic points. On the Main Assembly Lines were various inspection stages during the course of assembly, to ensure the correctness of assembly and the standard of workmanship, and a final inspection stage of the completed unit at the end of the bench. The inspector would then take the unit and place it in the Test Department racking ready for testing.

The Test department ran the length of the assembly building and was separated from the assembly area by a wide gangway and a length of shoulder high racking which prevented access to the Test department from the Assembly Area. The test benches, similar to the assembly ones, were in short rows and each bench was equipped with all the necessary test apparatus required for testing a particular type of unit. Thus, for example, the assembly line building transmitters would pass a completed unit, via inspection, to the transmitter test bench and so on.

Completely tested units were then passed to final inspection, supervised by an A.I.D. inspector, and then fitted into their cases and passed to packing and despatch. The A.I.D. (Aeronautical Inspection Directorate) had a number of resident inspectors at the factory. They, in fact, checked the work of the company's inspectors and all associated records, not 100% but random checks. Whilst they could not issue instructions to company's inspectors they could have an inspector removed from his job if it was considered his work was careless or inefficient. Perhaps one of the most dreaded situations was at the final inspection of units after test before fitting into cases. There was always an A.I.D. inspector at this stage and if he found a fault or bad workmanship, he would insist on a re-inspection of that complete batch of units. This inevitably meant working overtime to prevent a delay in despatch, an unforgivable sin. Completed and tested units were usually passed to final inspection in batches of twenty.

Where any electrical tests were required on sub assemblies, a test station would be set up at the appropriate position on the production line. The Coil Winding Department had its own extensive electrical testing facilities. All transformers were fully tested "in the white", that is, before varnish impregnation. Any rejects found at this stage could be sent back for rewinding. As full insulation tests could not be carried out before varnish impregnation transformers were tested a second time. Any rejects at this stage, and they were very rare, were scrapped because disassembly was impossible after varnishing.

Chapter 11
Further Problems

At about this time another major problem arose. The completely assembled and wired units went to final inspection and were then passed to the Test Department where valves were fitted. The Tester would then connect up and switch on and start testing and calibration procedures. In the majority of cases the set would work first time, if not then the tester would spend ten or fifteen minutes checking to find the fault.

If the fault could not be found in that time, the set would be put on one side into the "grave yard", and the tester would proceed to check the next unit. The reason for this was that the weekly despatch target had to be met and there was a limited time that could be spent on each unit. In slack times or when the assembly line was held up for some reason or other, the tester would then spend time clearing up his "grave yard" by finding the fault and sending the set back to be repaired.

Alarm bells started to ring when it was noted that "grave yards" were getting bigger and bigger and the number of equipments so held up was unacceptable. Overtime was therefore started to clear the backlog. The faults seemed obscure and difficult to trace and in some cases parts of the circuit heated up, and some components burned out. Eventually, one Tester noticing a resistor heating up, switched off and measured its value. This was found to be 10,000 ohms when its colour coding indicated that it should be 100,000 ohms (a factor of 10 out) This started a detailed check on all other types of equipment and it was found that in some cases resistors measuring 100,000 ohms were colour coded 10,000 ohms or 47,000 as 470,000 and so on. Immediately came the cry "It's Goods Inwards Inspection's fault". This department was immediately put on overtime and over 250,000 resistors were drawn out of Stores and each one re-tested. Not a single reject was found so, the mystery deepened.

Now tag board assemblies, to which resistors, capacitors, and other small components were assembled, wired up and the connections soldered, were made in the Small Parts Assembly Department, working to the coloured diagrams mentioned earlier. They were inspected and any that were incorrectly wired or fitted with the wrong components, or where the workmanship was poor were rejected and a label describing the fault was attached. Rejected assemblies of all types were passed to the Salvage Department who did what they could to repair these assemblies, or salvage undamaged components. In the case of incorrect components being fitted to tag boards, for example a wrong value resistor, then that resistor would be removed and the correct value fitted.

An example of this being that the inspector might tie a label round a resistor stating "should be brown body, black tip and yellow spot" where perhaps a 10,000 ohm resistor had been fitted instead of the 100,000 ohm which would have been correct. Neither the inspector nor the operators knew what resistors did, or what the colour codes meant. They just followed the coloured assembly charts mentioned earlier. Replacing a resistor on a tag board was no easy matter, because every soldered joint had to be "mechanically and electrically sound". That meant, all wire connections had to be tightly wrapped round the tag one and a half times and firmly clinched and then soldered. Removing a resistor was therefore difficult and there was a real danger of breaking the tag off and thereby scrapping the whole tag board.

One day a bright spark in the Salvage Department said, "If the spot is the wrong colour, let's paint it the right colour instead of changing the resistor. And so, it started. Now because of the obsession with security and the isolation of one department from another. The inspector in the Small Parts Assembly Department re-inspecting the repaired tag board did not know the incorrect resistor had not be replaced with the correct one, neither was he aware of the mayhem that existed in the Test Department. Thus the problems multiplied.

Note. Resistors are essential components of all Electronic Equipment. The Unit of resistance is the ohm or the Greek symbol Ω. Frequent resistors of high ohmic values are used, hence the terms Kilohm and Megohm. Resistors in those days were somewhat different and larger than those of today. A one watt resistor, the most commonly used type, consisted of a stick of carbon rod about 40 mm long and 8 mm in diameter and used the same colour coding as today, but in a different manner, in so far that the overall body colour was the first digit, the end tip was painted a different colour which represented the second digit and a spot on the body about 5 mm diameter indicates the number of 0s. The colour code was Black = 0, Brown = 1, Red = 2, Orange = 3 and Yellow = 4 etc. Thus a resistor having a brown body = 1, a black tip = 0 this =10, and an orange spot = 3 x 0s makes it's value 10,000 ohms (the unit of resistance).

If now, this 10,000 ohm resistor had its orange spot painted over yellow (=4 x 0s) it would still be a 10,000 ohm resistor but its colour code would indicate 100,000 ohms. Conversely if a 100,000 ohm resistor had its yellow spot painted over orange it would appear to be a 10,000 ohm resistor.

Wartime Resistors
(Actual size)
Showing how easy it is to change the
Colour of the spots

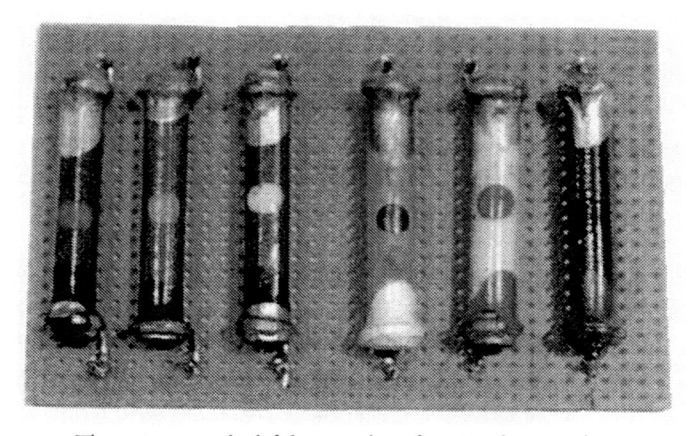

The resistor on the left has a value of 1,000 ohms. Red spot
The next one is 10,000 ohms. Orange spot
The third from the left is 100,000 ohms. Yellow spot.

A special "Point to Point" test was instituted after final inspection of the completed units and before valves were fitted. This test measured the resistance in the circuit from various points, to the chassis and to the HT line. In this way most of the rogue resistors were found, although at this stage it was still not known where they came from. Then one day the Chief of Test wandering round the factory went into the Salvage Department. Noticing a row of different coloured enamel paint tins in the windowsill asked, "What do you use those for?" "Oh", came the reply "painting resistors".

The Secret War Factory

At last the mystery was solved. It is said that a little knowledge can be dangerous, but no knowledge at all can be fatal!

Finally, the real source of the problem was found to be a girl on the Small Parts Assembly line who was colour blind and was unable to differentiate between the orange and yellow spots on the resistors. Discovering this had not been straightforward since there were "assemblers" and "solderers". The assemblers fitted the components to the tag board, after which it was passed to another girl who soldered the joints. About three assemblers fed one solderer. A batch of tag boards was then finally passed to inspection and at this stage it was by no means clear which girl had actually fitted the resisters to any particular panel.

Chapter 12
The Coil Winding Department

The original Winding Department was upstairs in the cottages overlooking the river. A Mr and Mrs Barrett ran the department although Mr Barrett was a chemist and looked after the Plating Department as well and spent most of his time there, showing little interest in the Winding Department leaving this to his wife, a platinum blond. She spent most of her time showing the girls different hairstyles and teaching them about make up. Consequently output from the department was only a fraction of what it should have been. At that time, owing to the shortage of Testers, I was on loan from the Test Apparatus Department and with two assistants was running the Winding Test Department.

Eventually a new large building was erected at the far end of the site near the Home Farm, about a quarter of a mile from the canteen. This caused some discontent amongst the girls as they were always last to arrive in the Canteen at meal times. This new building housed up to 100 operators and an enlarged Test Department.

The Barretts were dismissed and a Manager from one of the Ekco Aylesbury factories was installed as Superintendent of the Winding Department and was assisted by a foreman. In the following year he managed to turn the situation from chaos into total disaster! Half finished transformers were stacked everywhere and there was total disorganisation. Most assembly departments were now being held up owing to the shortage of transformers and coils. The problem here was not due to the operators, as most were highly skilled workers with an interest and pride in their work and they were not suffering from the machine Shop malaise, but the fault was due to the management. This Superintendent was sent on indefinite leave suffering from a nervous breakdown.

Drastic measurers were taken. More girls were employed, including a contingent of girls sent up from Devon and Cornwall, and a night shift started. The day shift worked from eight in the morning until eight in the evening, and the night shift the other twelve hours. Due to my experience of testing the output from the department it was assumed that I had some knowledge of coil winding, and I was roped in to run one shift. The shifts changed over each month so it was a month on nights followed by a month on days. Now each shift had a clerk whose job was to record the time each girl was spent working on a particular job and how many items she produced. The girls worked on a bonus scheme and the clerk's records were used to calculate her bonus earnings. I worked the first night shift and the foreman the second month. He then refused to work any more nights for reasons, which were never disclosed to me, but I had my own thoughts, which proved to be correct. The clerk, a very attractive girl, working on his night shift became pregnant and he, a confirmed bachelor, ended up marrying her. I was, therefore, lumbered with supervising the night shift for the next five months.

After transformer coils had been wound, laminations were assembled into the coils to complete the transformer. This was quite a skilful job and was commonly called lamming. One clerk, a country girl born and bred, would insist on writing down this operation as <u>lambing</u> on the girls' time sheets!

Eventually when production had caught up and there were sufficient stocks to ensure there were no more hold ups on the assembly lines, the night shift was abandoned and I was transferred to the Production Planning Department, which I eventually managed. Several crises of this nature occurred from time to time. The Machine Shop went through a phase where it had to run a night shift to catch up with production requirements. The most important thing was that nothing was allowed to delay the shipment of completed equipments from the factory.

Chapter 13
Other Departments

The Machine Shop and Main Assembly Departments were the two largest departments followed by the Winding Department that employed about one hundred girls. This was housed in a new purpose built brick building at the far northern end of the grounds, about a quarter of a mile from the canteen, which caused discontent among the girls, as they were always last to arrive at the canteen at meal times. Adjacent to the Winding Department was another building which incorporated the old original stables, (this was some distance from the new stables that formed part of the Machine Shop) this housed the Impregnation Department where all transformers and coils were vacuum impregnated in insulating varnish, most were also coated with a tropicalising compound. In the same building was the paint spraying and stoving ovens for parts that were painted. The electro-plating department was also located here. All steel parts were cadmium plated and brass and copper parts were silver-plated.

The Small Parts Assembly Department (SPA) occupied the first three long benches in the Main Assembly building. Here Tag Board assemblies and other sub assemblies were made for incorporation into the equipments assembled on the main assembly lines. A Salvage Department where faulty assemblies, which had been rejected by Inspection, were repaired. This was located in a large room off the main assembly building that was actually part of the old original house.

The remainder of the ground floor of the old house was occupied by the Main Stores, the Goods Inwards Inspection Department, the Purchasing Department and the Progress Chasers Office, along with the office of the Chief of Test and Inspection.

The first floor of the old house was used for office accommodation, wages, accounts administration, General Manager's office etc. The top floor consisted of a series of small rooms, originally the estate staff quarters, which were used as laboratories where prototype units were produced and Test Apparatus designed and made.

An additional new building adjoining the Machine Shop housed the Tool Room where highly skilled Toolmakers were employed. Here press tools, drilling jigs and other fixtures for the assembly departments were made. Over the Tool Room was a Drawing Office where the tools and fixtures were designed and drawn up. The Chief Mechanical Engineer's office was also located here.

Opposite the Machine Shop across the yard was the original Coach House, the ground floor of which was used as a Sheet metal stores. Upstairs was the Model Shop (Originally the Personnel Department) that produced parts and metal work for the Prototype and Test Apparatus Laboratories.

Beyond the Coach House, and encroaching into the kitchen gardens were two large wooden buildings, one housed the Production Engineering Department and the other the Production Planning Department. This latter was where a

The Secret War Factory

unit, such as a transmitter, for example, was broken down into assembly stages which would take about the same time to assemble for the main assembly lines as described earlier. Any assembly fixtures required were designed and drawn up here as were the water coloured drawings of tag boards to assist in their assembly. Two artists from the Manchester School of Art were employed for this purpose.

Across the yard from the side of the old house was a small brick built building with an elaborately carved door. Inside the panelled walls were decorated with carved Masonic symbols. The building was known as the Masonic Lodge. It was now used as the First Aid Centre where there was both a resident nurse and a doctor.

The entrance to the estate was down a curving drive so that the Main Gate could not be seen from the road. The security building was at the Main Gate through which all employees had to pass, showing their pass, to gain access. Above the Security House the Personnel Department was housed. This location was chosen so that prospective employees could be interviewed without entering the main factory.

Finally beside the Masonic Lodge was a flight of stairs down to a large lower area. On one side of the area was a large single story building housing the Maintenance Workshops. This comprised of electricians, plumbers, carpenters, bricklayers and fitters of all kinds to maintain, not only all the buildings and services, but also all the various machines used in the production departments. On the other side of this area was a row of cottages where the gardeners and pig keeper lived. When the company first purchased the estate they retained the services of these men, so that the kitchen gardens and piggery could remain productive to supply the canteen.

Chapter 14
Security

Our security Guards were housed in a large guardhouse located at the main gate. To gain admission one had to walk through a passageway in the guardhouse past a large counter where the guards were located. Officially this was the way we should enter showing our passes as we went through. Only two at a time could enter this way. This, of course, was totally impractical at eight in the morning when masses were pushing to get in and clock in before three minutes past eight. So the main gate was opened to let the hoard through with one security guard on each side scanning for faces that should not have been there!!

All the security guards were ex police officers well educated and well spoken. I think they must all have been well above the rank of constable when in the force. They all seemed to have a remarkable memory for faces. There was always a minimum of four on duty on days and at least five at night.

The work of our security guards was there for all to see, but incidents occurred which showed that others outside of the factory were also involved with security. Not everyone witnessed or experienced these incidents. I will give some illustrations of what I mean. There must have been many other instances, which were unknown to me. It was not until after the war that

I knew that after the Regular Army guards moved out, the RAF Security Unit took responsibility and they made regular attempts to break into the grounds and buildings to test our internal security.

Home Farm was located beyond the Factory grounds, to the north and the entrance to the factory gate was located on the south boundary. The farm also had land further to the south and at haymaking and harvest times the crops had to be hauled, usually by horse and cart through the factory grounds to the farm. This was quite a distance as the factory grounds were 14 acres in extent.

One evening I went on guard duty with a fellow who happened to be a farmer's son. It was after eight o'clock and still extremely bright, because during the war years the introduction of double summer time meant that on a sunny day it would stay quite bright until 10 0'clock. As we stood there a horse and cart came rumbling up the drive with hay on board. The security guard opened the gate to admit the cart and as it came in my mate shouted "Halt" which the driver did. My mate said to me, "That is not a proper load of hay" and then in a loud voice said, "Stick you bayonet into that hay it doesn't look right" and low and behold a man came scrambling out from under the hay. The guard who was still by the gate immediately arrested him. It transpired he was from the RAF Security Unit trying to gain access to the factory. My mate earned many a pint from all of us on duty that night because of his observance. We all shuddered to think of the wrath our Commanding Officer would bestow upon us had he got through. He was short tempered at the best of times. We also sent the farmer a strong letter complaining bitterly about his worker's treachery. Later my fellow guard said to me nobody would send a horse and cart from the fields to the farm with the couple of handfuls of hay that were on board.

The Secret War Factory

It was not a point I, or possibly any of the others, would have appreciated either, had it been down to us.

On another occasion when I was working on the Night Shift in the Coil Winding Department, Sam, who was working in the Plating Shop, had nipped out into the yard for a smoke. It was a bright moonlit night when he looked up the road and saw Reg., our night shift electrician, walking into the telephone exchange and as he looked he saw someone following him. He knew there shouldn't be anyone else there so he rushed inside and grabbed a heavy spanner and ran up the road rushing into the telephone exchange. There he saw Reg. arguing with this man who wanted to use the phone. When Sam threatened him with his spanner he came quietly and they took him up to the gatehouse where the police arrested him. Again it proved to be the RAF Security Unit trying to break in.

When I started to work nights, on the first night the telephone in my office rang at about eight thirty. I thought it must be my wife and when I answered it was an attractive feminine voice but not my wife. The voice said,
"This is the RAF Security Service, please identify yourself". After this she went on "As the most senior on site you are responsible for the site, we know your location is farthest from the Security Guards station but if you see or hear anything you are unhappy about ring your Security Guards immediately". After swapping a few more niceties She said "I will ring you again between two and two thirty, Remember these calls are confidential and make sure you keep it that way".

She did just that asking me what I had had for dinner and was it nice, how was the weather etc. This happened without fail every night although the times of ringing varied each night. In a way it was nice to know that someone out there cared.

CHAPTER 15
The Home Guard Unit

From the beginning, a platoon of soldiers camped in the grounds and formed a twenty four hour armed guard at the entrance gate, and also patrolled the grounds. This seemed to aggravate the local population even further and they commented in their local vernacular "They soldiers should be out fighting the war not mollycoddling that lot down at Cowbridge House". After the capitulation of France in June 1940 the soldiers, returned to their unit and the responsibility of guarding the factory passed from the Army to the RAF. They insisted that a Home guard Unit was formed and this was organized by Mr. H, an ex Guardsman, who was responsible for factory security. He became Captain and we had to guard the factory and grounds from eight pm until eight am. The increased security staff acted as guards during daytime.

The Ekco home guard detachment – photo from the S Day collection

Now there was the minimum number of able bodied men employed at the factory, although the Inspection Department employed a number of disabled men. To meet the minimum requirements, two armed guards had to be on duty all night, watching the main gate and patrolling the grounds. Following the usual army practice, guard duty meant two hours on and four hours off. There were ten men and a sergeant on duty each night including weekends. Due to the shortage of men this meant that each of us had to be on duty every fifth night. The routine was finish work at eight pm, change into battle dress, draw a rifle and ammunition from the armoury and report for duty. At eight am rifles were put away, battle dress was discarded and it was back to work. Now this all happened very quickly and was organised in a great rush because we were given no warning that this was a likely move. The soldiers had gone and there was therefore no night security. For the first month, guards were on duty without any training and having never before handled a rifle, let alone fire one.

The Secret War Factory

The Guardroom was one of the old, original buildings and was probably used by the outside staff, gardeners, farm workers and the like as a mess room and store. It was now refurnished with six two tier bunk beds, table and chairs and large cupboards where we kept our daytime clothing. There were two further smaller rooms one was used as the Armoury where guns and ammunition were stored and the other was used as an office by the Maintenance Manager.

Quite early on, before our preliminary training had been completed, an incident occurred which thereafter made us all particularly wary where firearms were concerned One night, when two guards came back to the guardroom after their two hours on duty, they went through the normal routine of unloading their rifles, making the gun safe and storing the ammunition. It is uncertain as to what actually went wrong but one of them let off a shot, which penetrated a filing cabinet outside the Manager's Office. Thank goodness he was facing that way. Nobody was hurt but the noise caused the rest to leap out of their beds in total shock. What seems remarkable is that when the filing cabinet draw was prised open the bullet had gone round and round in the papers chewing them up and forming a massive nest and the bullet was still sitting there in the middle. After that no one ever saw a rifle being carelessly handled.

Training was compulsory every Sunday morning at ten am, so we had lost the only day we had for a morning in bed! Regular soldiers were there to show us how to handle a rifle and bayonet. We had much bayonet practice stabbing dummies, (sacks stuffed with straw). The issue was five rounds of ammunition each to practice firing on the range. We also spent hours practising throwing hand grenades with an over arm lob. The day came when we had to throw two live grenades, to get our proficiency badge. We went one at a time into a dug out with the sergeant instructor to throw our grenades. One enthusiast asked, "Where is the target sarg", "Never mind about a target", he said, "just throw the b….y thing as far as you can."

The manager of the Wages Department was a short, dapper little man, very ambitious in the home guard and by some means or other got himself promoted to lieutenant. He scoured all the local towns until he managed to find a pair of brown boots. Home Guard officers were not issued with brown boots. Apart from his stature, his other problem was his inability to pronounce his R's. There was many a titter when he ordered, "Stand Easy and West your Wifles!

Eventually we were issued with Sten Guns and what lethal things they were! We had many unfortunate incidents with these and it was a miracle that no blood was spilt. We never had permission to take a Sten gun on guard duty. The Lewis Gun was another questionable asset. We spent hours learning how to strip and reassemble the thing, but never had enough ammunition to use it even in practice.

Once the novelty had worn off, the Home Guard training sessions were felt as another imposition and the number of volunteers for working overtime on Sunday mornings escalated, anything to get out of the training sessions. At least one was paid for working overtime. Others tried getting medical certificates for some reason or the other, but the local doctors wouldn't play ball!

Chapter 16
The Canteen

Food and meal times occupied a good deal of attention, and the girls eat a noticeably large amount, considering the inactive nature of their work. For instance, a girl working in the machine shop usually had a hot breakfast before she left home in the morning; at ten o'clock she had tea and cheese rolls; at one o'clock there was dinner – meat and vegetables and pudding; at six o' clock there was high tea - cheese and potato pie, or fish cakes or something like that - and then usually a hot supper when she got back in the evening. And in addition to this, most of them brought cakes and sandwiches to eat at odd times during the morning or more often during the four-hour stretch in the afternoon.

There seemed to be a definite relation between boredom and this large consumption of food. Eating makes a change and relief from monotony as nothing else does. Even if one is not hungry, it is a great relief during the long afternoon to have a piece of cake to look forward to; to be able to say to oneself, at four o'clock I'm going to stop and eat my cake. It makes a sort of landmark to look forward to and plan about, which is difficult with all other kinds of slacking, most of which just happens without the possibility of plan. At break times, going up to the canteen makes much more of a change than just staying in the

Charles Exton

work room, and once you are in the canteen the obvious thing to do is to have something to eat and drink.

The original estate included a large kitchen garden and the Company had the foresight to retain the services of the head gardener and two under gardeners, along with the groom who had looked after the pigs.

As a result the canteen was adequately supplied with all their needs for fresh vegetables and some fruit and the canteen waste fattened the pigs. Tons of potatoes and carrots were grown and carrots appeared daily on the menu, either as vegetables or carrot pudding or carrot cake. The pigs provided a plentiful supply of meat and ham, cured locally, along with fresh lettuce and tomatoes, which made a salad that could not be bettered anywhere.

The garden in Wartime

This was all due to the organisation and planning of Miss N. who ruled the canteen and its staff with a rod of iron.

The Secret War Factory

Nevertheless she was popular with her staff. Previously she had been responsible for the catering at a large women's prison!

Though the quality of the food was, on the whole, fairly well appreciated, there were also a number of vigorous complainers. The complaints are not usually very specific, but embraced the whole canteen food, staff and organisation in one breath. The fact that the complaints heard in the main are so sweeping and so obviously emotive in tone, leads one to suspect that their basis is psychological rather then material. From this standpoint, there seemed to be three main factors at work.

The first appeared most strongly in people who are resenting being in the factory at all. Their unwillingness to come here and their dislike of the work leads them to dislike indiscriminately anything to do with factory life, and they vent this feeling on any aspect of the life which is in their power to reject, food is one of the few things there which comes into this category.

The second factor was simple snobbishness, and appeared more among women than men. Girls were pretending (to themselves quite as much as to anyone else) that they had come from more prosperous homes than they had, tended to hammer in this impression by belittling the food they got away from home in comparison with the food they got at home.

The third attitude, which in a sense was a more genuine one, was found among the poorer classes. The reason for objection was that they are genuinely unaccustomed to that type of food. A woman who was accustomed to making her dinner off a couple of slices of bread and margarine with a taste of pickles or sausage, did not know quite what to make of a plate of steamed fish with a strange sauce over it, and some dark coloured beans that she had never seen before in her life. The line of least resistance when confronted with this apparition was to call it "muck", and bring sandwiches filled with her familiar brawn.

Of genuine complaints about specific material points there appeared to be very few. As one shop steward put it "Well, people must have something to grumble about, and next to the weather, food is the most universal target. It's just a safety valve like the speakers in Hyde Park". The only two specific complaints at all frequently heard, are that the washing up is not good enough, and (rather vaguely) that people push into the front of the queue out of turn. As indeed they did, but it was difficult to know how to prevent this, except by force of public opinion. Of course there were a number of complaints based on personal likes and dislikes – "The meat's overdone", "The meat's underdone", I don't like rice pudding", and so on.

Apart from the washing–up, there was very little to be altered in the canteen with any advantage. For the bulk of complaints were based on a psychological situation with which it is no part of a cook's business to cope.

Chapter 17
Leisure Time

What of the leisure time, which amounted to Saturday afternoons and Sundays chiefly. "There's nothing to do in this dump". This is a phrase heard over and over again, from soldiers, from factory workers, from Air Ministry employees – from every one in fact, who had been brought in to the town, more or less involuntarily, for the duration of the war. And a walk through the town on a Sunday afternoon would, superficially, lend weight to this complaint. At every corner there were knots of soldiers, just standing. Some were smoking and some, not even doing that, others just strolling languidly up and down outside the Y.M.C.A. where they were billeted. Though they were in less evidence, the situation was much the same with the girl factory workers, Some of them were to be seen wandering about the streets in twos or threes, aimlessly, and in no special direction, but an even greater number were just sitting in their billets, with no household jobs to occupy them, idling over a piece of mending, or writing a letter. And the reason given for all this lack of definite occupation was the same – "There's nothing to do".

Now, to some extent this was probably the natural reaction of a town dweller to be transported to a small country town rural in nature where there was no ready-made entertainment.

In Malmesbury, any entertainment 'as was' had to be self made and for a lot of people this was alien to their nature having been used to finding entertainment ready-made. The problem was that a very big proportion of this imported population had no intention of adapting. They knew they were only temporarily displaced; they also knew that, after a shorter or longer period of time, they would leave and never see it again. There was thus an overpowering atmosphere of, "it's not worth bothering", which hung like a pail over any attempt to organise social activities of any kind, other than standard entertainments like cinemas and dances, to which one could go mechanically and from habit, without any mental or emotional effort.

These were the only two kinds of social activity for which there was anything approaching a popular demand, and of these, it was only the cinema that was really well attended. There was only one cinema in the town, and it was quite small. The show was changed twice a week and on Sunday evenings there was a special programme put on by the factory authorities themselves, as mentioned earlier. There was always a long queue for every showing during the weekend, particularly on Saturday evenings. This caused some resentment amongst the locals.

> "We didn't ought to have to wait like this. They ought to let us in first; we've lived here all our lives, and let the others wait. Pushing in front like they do, and I don't suppose they knew there was such a place as Malmesbury six weeks ago".

The cinema was the one event that the factory girls really could look forward to and enjoy. There was always a lot of talk about films as the weekend approached, and going formed a sort of focal point to an otherwise aimless and drifting weekend. There were of course a few complaints from them about queuing, which some of them seemed to quite enjoy.

> "Let's get there real early tonight and see who's there. We could get some fish and chips and stand there and eat them while they're all hot and nice. You can't really eat them when you're pushing in, can you?

There was quite a big selection of available dances. The Catholic School (which has a good sized hall) held dances on Mondays, Thursdays and Saturdays; the Social Centre Saturdays and Sundays. The intervening days were frequently filled up by odd dances, held by the R.A.M.C., or by some other section of the local Forces. On special occasions the Town Hall was used.

Most of them were fairly well attended, but not very lively affairs. There were inevitably many more girls than men, and the men who were there tended to hang about in corners and not dance; many of them having come simply for the universal reason "there's nothing to do". By about ten, when the pubs shut, things usually began to warm up a bit, but even then there was not the atmosphere of real, wholehearted enjoyment that one usually got at working-class dances. The reason for this is, of course, that so many of them went simply because they could think of nothing better to do. They had no strong desire to make friends – one of the most usual reasons for going to dances – because so many of them felt that they were only going to be in Malmesbury for a short time, they had all their friends at home; and all their interests were focused on counting the days till next weekend, when they could go home.

The Social Centre was ideally situated in the centre of the town and catered primarily, of course, for newcomers to the town although membership was open to anyone, whether working at the factory or not. The authorities did not take into account

Charles Exton

(indeed, it would have been hard to foretell it beforehand) the aloof and disinterested attitude that so many newcomers were going to adopt to their whole life in Malmesbury. Instead of settling down to build up a new life and circle of friends, workers pushed into the town by circumstances or force, firmly maintained all their home interests and friends; their home was still the only real life to them, and the displacement merely an irritating or distressing interlude, to be got through as quickly as possible. A number of remarks about the Social Centre illustrate, directly and indirectly, this attitude:
"I wouldn't trouble myself to go there. I don't care about factory girls, and I wouldn't trouble myself to trail round there just on the chance of making friends".

> "I think it's very nice, what I've heard of it. And if I were really living here I'd expect I'd go. But I can get home most weekends, so it wouldn't be worth my while joining".
> "They only go there to try and find a young man, most of them. I've got my young man up in Yorkshire, I don't want to go hunting round for more".
> I don't know, I'm not very interested. I'm not very interested in this place at all".

This attitude towards social life of any kind was a fundamental problem, and there was no organisation, or programme changes at he Social Centre, which could have had any effect on it all. Far deeper and more radical changes in the whole structure of wartime life would have been needed, quite outside the scope of any single locality or organisation. It is interesting, however, to consider a few minor points in this Social Centre that detracted from its popularity.

In the first place, the fact that it was organised and sponsored by the factory management and that they were often to be found there, was one, which could not forgotten. Many lower grade employees felt shy of meeting any of their bosses "out of school" as are school children of meeting their masters and mistresses. A lot of reasons for not joining seem to hinged on this.

> "The Social Club? Isn't that where Mr. G (Welfare Manager) and all of them go? I wouldn't like to go in there".
> "I'd be scared. I'd be scared I'd meet Mr. L (Manager) there".
> Closely allied to this, is the feeling among many, e.g. the machine-shop employees, that it is the exclusive preserve of the office staff;
> "Oh no. I don't belong. It's for the office girls really".
> "Well you have to be a bit posh to go there, don't you"?
> "I wouldn't go in there, with all them snobs from the office. I'd rather go to an ordinary dance".

In fact, it was mainly office staff and higher grade employees who went there, although this was contrary to the original idea of the place. Another thing was that the small number of people who habitually went there got to know each other so well that any newcomer tended to feel rather out of it.

> "I've been round there two or three times but they're funny in there. So stand-offish. I poked my nose in there on Saturday night, but I soon brought it out again. They were all sitting round the walls whispering, and nobody spoke to me. It was miserable".
> "They're all such a clique there, all in together".
> "I don't like going in there. I've only been once or twice, and they look at you as if they wonder why you are there".
> "I can't go. I don't know anybody.

Charles Exton

These, then, were about the sum of social activities. Attempts to organise anything further, like dramatic groups, cycling or walking clubs, and so on – all at the very outset ran up against the same barrier – lack of lively demand for such activities, due to total lack of interest.

CHAPTER 18
The New Centimetric Airborne Radar

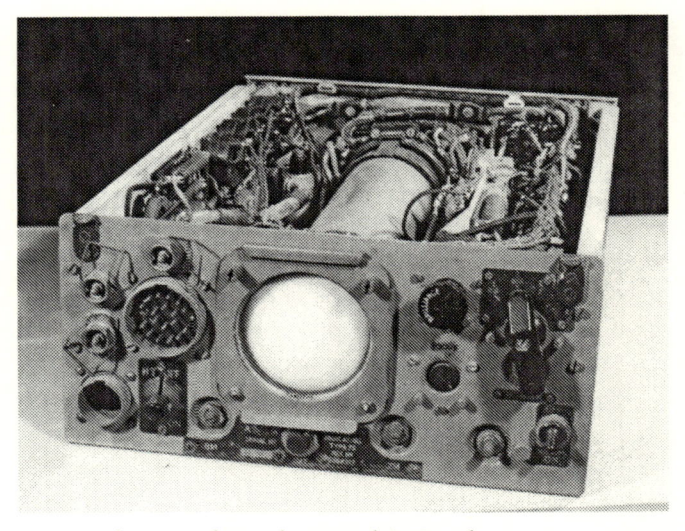

Ekco manufactured AI-Mark VIII indicator unit.

To return to the real purpose of the factory, the production of airborne radar equipment. Towards the end of 1941 news came that a new system know as AI Mk VII was in the pipeline. This was to be the first equipment to use the Magnetron in the transmitter with a reflecting klystron as a local oscillator with a crystal mixer in the receiver, all for the new 10cm wavelength system. These new techniques would require different production testing equipment and methods.

Shortly afterwards it was confirmed that AI Mk VIII was to be the version that would go into production and, after prototype approval, an initial contract for 1,000 systems was received. It was understood that testing would be more sophisticated than hitherto. In the final testing, all units would be connected together to form a complete installation and then "air tested", transmitting to a known target. For this a test tower within the factory grounds would have to be built and a corresponding target erected about two miles away,

The only item of the complete system not to be produced by E.K.Cole was the aerial system. This was a complex piece of mechanism developed by the Telecommunications Research Establishment (TRE) and Nash and Thompson who became the exclusive manufacturer. Driven by an hydraulic motor, not only did the aerial dipole revolve but also the "dish", about 30 ins diameter, which oscillated radially at the same time to give the unique radial scan. This assembly rotated at 360 r.p.m. When not installed in an aircraft and it was frightening to watch. One marvelled that pieces were not flying off all over the place!

The Secret War Factory

Mark VIII Nash and Thompson scanner unit in nose of Beaufighter

The site for the location of the target was not an easy matter as Cowbridge House and grounds are located at the bottom of a narrow valley on the banks of the river Avon, which flows roughly north to south. To the west the valley rises steeply up Cowbridge Hill but less steeply to the east. To the north, up the valley, was Home Farm with several high metal barns and other clutter. The best possibility seemed to be to the south.

Some experiments were started in which I became involved. AI Mk VII Units were dragged up on to the roof of Cowbridge House and the horizon to the south was scanned for a suitable site for the target. A spot was selected across the fields about 1,500 yards (1372 metres) away. The target was a tinplate pyramid about three feet square (0.91 meters) and three feet to the apex. On a lovely summer day we set off across the fields with two long ladders, a lot of rope and the target. Two or three times we stopped and looked back at our chief on the roof and each time his frantic arm waving indicated that we go on further. Finally we arrived at the chosen spot and erected the two ladders to form an inverted V and securely roped them in place, fixing the target at the top. We trudged back, exhausted,

Charles Exton

and up on to the roof where we found our chief peering through the rangefinder and swearing loudly. Picking up the binoculars I was horrified to see a farm tractor and trailer drawn up beside our target and the farmer pulling it down and loading the ladders and rope on to his trailer and then driving off into the sunset! Actually the technical needs for this project were beyond our current knowledge and we had more pressing duties waiting, so thankfully the task was undertaken by T.R.E. and our W.D.U. (Western Development Unit).

So, by the autumn of 1942, a test tower was built in the north-east corner of the grounds. A steel framework clad with corrugated iron about fifteen feet (4.57 meters) square and eighty feet (24.38 metres) high. There was only one floor and that was about seven feet (2.13 metres) from the top, to which access was gained by an open steel spiral stairway running round the four walls. A small electric hoist took units for testing up to this top floor.

A complete AI Mk VIII system was installed on a bench about twelve feet (3.65 metres) long, each unit being inter-connected with actual aircraft installation cables to simulate operational conditions. The aerial dish pointed out through a large Perspex window at the target. A security guard was posted at the bottom of the tower and a special pass was needed to gain access. Each unit, after final production, test was brought to the tower and fitted into the standard system for operational test. For example, a receiver coming in for test would be connected up into the system in place of the "standard" receiver and a system test completed. If the next unit to be tested was a modulator, the "standard" receiver would be replaced into the system and the modulator for test would replace the "standard" modulator, and so on.

The target was a seventy-foot (21.34 metres) high mast about two miles (3.22 Km) or so away to the northeast on farm land, just outside of the village of Garsden. It was just visible from the top of the test tower under good weather conditions. Even in wartime one could not escape red tape, here we have a seventy feet high (21.34 metres) mast, owned by the RAF and loaned to E.K.Cole but erected by T.R.E. Now who was responsible for erecting a fence around it to prevent grazing cattle from stumbling into the guy ropes and bringing the whole thing down? Not the RAF, not E.K.Cole, not T.R.E. After weeks of deliberation it was found to be the responsibility of the Directorate of Works at the Air Ministry and the fencing was finally put up in February 1943. End of story? Not quite. A storm in April blew it down and the saga started all over again!

The rigorous testing schedule for each unit of the system included the equivalent to high altitude flying conditions, vibration testing and now air testing with the units connected together with an actual aircraft wiring loom which meant, that when leaving the factory, units could be installed directly into operational aircraft. Whereas previously, equipment had to be flight-tested before going into service, which increased cost and the time before equipment went into service.

Every new equipment design had its teething problems and A.I. Mk. VIII was no exception. A standard test for every kind of airborne equipment produced was the "Tank Test". For this test the equipment is put into a large heavy steel tank, connected up and made fully operational. The Tank is then closed and the air evacuated down to a specific level of vacuum. The equipment was then switched on and carefully observed through windows in the tank to see if there was any high voltage arcing or breakdown and the performance of the unit was also checked to ensure that no deterioration had occurred. This test was to simulate the condition of flying at a high altitude.

The decision that Mk. VIII should have a ceiling of 35,000 feet was received with some apprehension, as this was 10.000 feet higher than usual with previous equipment. This was because Mk. VIII was to be fitted to the Mosquito as well as the Beaufighter which had a normal ceiling of 25,000 feet, 2,000 feet is added to the desired ceiling to give a safety margin and at 37,000 feet the temperature can fall as low as -60°C. Temperature was therefore a critical figure when calculating tank pressure. The main problem was whether, at that altitude, the temperature inside the equipment would fall below zero or not, as normally the valves and other components which run hot will maintain the temperature within the units when they are subjected to a temperature of -40°C which is expected at the lower altitude. Eventually a tank pressure of 190 mm of mercury at 15°C was agreed and subsequent tests proved that the equipment remained happy at this pressure, although some modifications were required to some units.

One such unit was the PU225 power unit. The transformer supplying the voltage to the heater filaments of the two high voltage rectifier valves, one handling + 8 Kilovolts and the other – 9 Kilovolts was, under tank test, arcing between one set of windings and another set of windings, and between the windings and the laminated iron core. This necessitated a redesign of the transformer in rather a novel way. Each heater winding was encapsulated in neoprene, rather like a miniature ring doughnut before assembling them to the primary winding.

Another more serious problem involved the Modulator output pulse transformer and the Transmitter input pulse transformer. These two units, when fitted in an aircraft are connected together by a relatively long cable. The functions of these two transformers are to reduce the output impedance of the Modulator for the transmission of the pulses through the cable and to bring the impedance up again with the transformer in the Transmitter. Without going into too much detail, suffice to say, that during the winding of the transformer, a slippage of one layer of windings into the previous layer, due to the slippery nature of the bobbin, increased the self capacity of the transformer sufficiently to distort the pulse wave-shape during its transmission through the inter connecting cable. A new transformer winding technique had to be developed. The other contractor producing AI MK VIII was GEC and they never resolved the pulse transformer winding problems so E.K.Cole manufactured pulse transformers for them.

CHAPTER 19
Finale

Now where was I in all this? After my initial working through all the Production Departments I started work in the Test Department and quickly was made responsible for all final testing and later I was selected to be moved into the Test Apparatus Department, designing and building the specialised testing equipment required. From there I was loaned to the Coil Winding Department running the Testing Facility there. And, as has been told elsewhere, I ended up managing the Night Shift not only of the Winding Department but also the Plating Shop and the Paint Spraying Department. The Increased output from the Machine Shop necessitated the finishing Department to work nights.

And so it was that for five months I toiled from eight in the evening until eight in the morning until production became such that the night shift could be discontinued. My worst recollection of that time was shepherding seventy girls and twelve men from that group of buildings in pitch darkness, because of the blackout restrictions, the quarter mile distance to the canteen in the main building for the one to two am lunch break. Frequently there was a red alert (air raid warning) and not even our one torch was allowed as we groped our way up towards the canteen listening to the drone of German aircraft overhead.

Now for my own personal problems. My fiancé, who was secretary to the Chief of Test and Engineering, and I had been planning to get married and the timing happened to coincide with the start of the night shift. The Company gave us three days leave and allocated us a flat in one of the houses they had converted. The flat was in Sherston Manor, which was owned by Lady Douglas. She had moved out into another of her properties, Badminton House of Badminton Horse Trials fame. Sherston is a village about seven miles from Malmesbury and the company ran a bus service to and from the factory as a number of employees also lived in Sherston and the surrounding villages. On return from our two-day honeymoon we moved into the flat. The next morning my wife caught the works bus at 7.40 am to be into work for 8.00. I caught a bus in the evening to get me to work at 8pm to work on the night shift, and my wife caught the same bus back to take her home. In the morning as she caught the bus to go to work and I got on the same bus to go back home and get some sleep. For five days the only times we met was when we were getting on and off buses! Sundays were the only day we had together. This went on for five months. The joys of married life.

Despite all the problems, what was achieved? In 1939, 300 sets of AI (Aircraft Interception, carried in fighter aircraft) MK II and 300 sets of ASV (Air to Surface Vessel, carried in Coastal Command aircraft) Mk I. In 1940 3,000 sets of AI Mks III and IV. and 3,000 sets of ASV Mk II. Similar quantities of both types were produced in 1941. An unknown number of these were diverted to Naval and Army use e.g. for use in Naval types 286 and 271N and for the Army for use in Searchlight sets SLC (Elsie). From 1942 on AI Mk VIII was the main equipment produced and the first of these was despatched in

The Secret War Factory

December 1942. Several thousands of various Test Sets were also manufactured over the following years. At peak production times up to 100 units were being despatched daily. Pye Radio and EMI also manufactured AI equipment and Pye Radio also manufactured ASV Units.

It is a great pity that the significance of these production figures was not meaningful to the vast majority of the employees. Less than 5% of employees knew the purpose of the equipment and they were sworn to secrecy. Many high ranking officers from all three armed forces frequently visited the factory to give "Pep" talks during lunch breaks stressing the importance of the work at the factory without, of course, even hinting at the true nature of the production. It was generally accepted that the equipment was something to do with radio, but if it were communication equipment why not say so because surely such equipment was not so highly secret. It was obviously equipment for the Air Force since RAF lorries arrived daily to collect equipment from the Despatch Department.

Workers in aircraft and armament factories knew the significance of their efforts and could feel an enthusiasm for their work for the war effort, but at Malmesbury one can, perhaps, understand why this enthusiasm was largely lacking, as not knowing whether their long hours of work were really helping the war effort or not, was more than just irksome. The extent of this feeling can, perhaps be best illustrated by the fact that on the day after VJ Day very many of the skilled workers, such as Toolmakers Engineers and Technicians, did not turn up for work any more but returned to their original homes in various parts of the country.

Since production was almost completely halted for a time and the urgency was off, this did not cause a problem. The whole operation was completely reorganised as radar production slowed down, although AI Mk IX and AI Mk X trickled through but this was the American SCR 720 equipment, which we modified for the RAF. We were now entering the nuclear age with all the fears of a possible nuclear attack. The factory now, in conjunction with T.R.E. at Malvern, became involved with the development and production of nuclear instrumentation, including Dose Rate Meters. These were for distribution to Air Raid Wardens to measure radiation after an attack and measure out danger areas. Contracts were also received for Army communications equipment, the No. 88 haversack set, the most advanced "walkie talkie" set available and several thousands of these went into production.

Chapter 20
Bits and Pieces

We were all asleep in our dormitories in Rodbourne House Hostel when we were awakened by a German Bomber aircraft flying around very low. German Bombers were easily recognised by the drone of their engines. This particular aircraft seemed to be flying round and round. Suddenly there was a terrific roar and a loud thud that shook the whole house. The plane then flew off. Someone said "That was close" but we all went back to sleep.

In the morning when we went outside and on the other side of the drive was an enormous crater, and further over were two more. Looking down onto the crater the rear fins of one of the bombs could be clearly seen. By some miracle it had not exploded. Les rushed back in to telephone the police, Les stammered at the best of times, but now he was reduced to stuttering gibberish, fortunately Norman grabbed the phone and reported the matter.

About twenty or so minutes later PC Plod arrived on his bicycle and after looking into the crater telephoned the Bomb Disposal Squad, who arrived very quickly. They immediately evacuated the house telling us to quickly pack enough to last us for at least a week and go and walk down the lane for about a mile and wait until we were picked up by the factory lorry. An upper floor of a warehouse in Malmesbury was quickly cleared and sleeping bags obtained from the emergency stores and we were installed.

Bomb disposal just after the bomb had been dug out – photo from the Sykes-Lipman collection

It took the Bomb Disposal boys more than a week to dig the bombs out and make them safe. It was considered that it was probably a stick of three that the aircraft was carrying and that he had lost his way to his target and just dumped them. It could not possibly be conceived that Rodbourne House was the target. The bombs were then transported to Malmesbury Common some five miles out of the town where they were exploded. The noise and reverberations could be heard and felt in the town.

Meanwhile we enjoyed ten days living in Malmesbury and enjoying the local pubs and cinema before being moved back to

The Secret War Factory

Rodborne House. It was very gratifying to see how quickly and efficiently the Emergency Services responded to the situation.

We had been living, compulsorily, about three miles from the factory at Rodbourne House for about two years when the Company relented and announced that those that wanted to could move out into other lodgings. About half a dozen immediately moved into lodgings in Malmesbury where there were many pubs (but not much beer), and the cinema at weekends. This greatly relieved the pressure on the bathroom at Rodbourne House.

Since I had a small motorbike for the journey to the factory I was not in a rush to leave. The lights on the bike were of course reduced to a glimmer due to the blackout regulations but I reckoned I knew the lanes pretty well. One very dark night on the way back Wham! I hit something solid but soft and went flying over the handlebars and the obstacle in the road. A loud braying told me I had hit a donkey that had been standing in the road but then quickly made off across the field. I was not hurt, just shaken and decided that maybe a move into Malmesbury might not be a bad thing.

On the following Saturday afternoon Cyril, who also wanted to move from Rodbourne, and I went to a small cottage in Bristol Street, Malmesbury where we had learned there was available accommodation. This turned out to be a small attic room sparsely furnished with two single beds and not much else. The Landlady, a widow, already had one lodger, Archie, a policeman. We felt we had to start somewhere so we took the room. We moved out of Rodbourne with our stuff now piled up in our attic room. It was bitterly cold at night. The water in our mugs was solid ice in the morning. There was a 'rag' wool rug on the floor and we took it in turns to have it on our beds at night.

A week or so later, on a Saturday night, we were sitting downstairs by the fire writing letters. Cyril said he would go out and post them later. Archie said "will you post one for me as well as I have to go on duty now". In due course Cyril set off on his bike, no lights of course, for the post office. On the way back he was stopped by Archie, who was on duty now, and he reported him for riding a bike without lights. Cyril was fined five shillings at the local court. This was enough for us and we left. We both found better accommodation but not together.

After all the men had moved out of Rodborne House it was refurbished and used as a female hostel, only they were given transport to and from the factory whereas we had to make our own way as best we could.

The National Services Act of 1941 which identified 'Mobile' women affected all women irrespective of Class or Creed. Lady D was so directed to the Malmesbury factory. She worked in the Accounts Department. The Accounts office was long and narrow with a door at each end. Mr G. the deputy General Manager had made a habit of going through the Accounts office as a short cut to his own office. In variably he left the door open and this upset Lady D. She would call out in a loud voice "Will you please close the door Mr G". This became almost a daily occurrence. One day she was exasperated and said in an equally loud voice "Before the war, people like us used to throw pennies for people like him". Mr G. left the office with a face flushed bright crimson. This had two effects, one, Mr G never took a shot cut through the Accounts Office again and two, the ice between Lady D and the rest of the office staff was broken and all became friends.

One day in the Test Department the foreman brought in a new recruit. He was introduced to us as Mr Ramsden-Binks. He was a very good looking young man and had been invalided out

The Secret War Factory

of the RAF. He was rather aloof and superior in manner and was reluctant to talk of his past. We did not take to him, but he had no difficulty in chatting up the girls on the assembly lines. He kept an RAF uniform jacket, stripped of its insignia, on the back of his chair. He was technically competent and worked, well but was not one of us. One morning one of our Security Guards came into the department accompanied by two large tall men and they went over to Ramsden-Binks and after a few words escorted him out. All we could get out of our Security man was that the other men were police officers. Whether it was just a case of the police catching up with a criminal, or whether it was something more sinister we never knew but suspected the later however. We never saw him again and we missed the extra pair of hands because we were always short handed but we were glad to see the back of him. One of the assembly girls nicked his uniform jacket.

With the exception of the gardening staff the Kitchen Gardens were strictly out of bounds to everyone, particularly to the Home Guard when they were on Guard Duty at night. However, in the early summer months with the strawberry plants, raspberry canes and gooseberry bushes bursting with fruit, for those on Guard Duty between 4am until 6am the temptation could not be resisted. The Head Gardener protested bitterly to our Captain that the Home Guards were stealing his fruit. "How do you know?" asked the Captain "By the footprints", he replied, "How do you know they are Home Guard footprints? they may be have been made by your own men earlier in the day." The crafty gardeners soon cured this. They took a load of ashes from the boiler house and scattered them over all the paths. The last gardener to leave at night walked backwards down the paths racking the ashes as he went. The result was smooth virgin path surfaces. The Head gardener said "If there is a footprint in the morning then it will have been made by a Home Guard".

Jock worked in the Inspection Department and was our favourite Scot. He was a big bear of a man and although he had an artificial leg he managed to get around fairly well. It had been a very hot sultry week and on the Friday evening Jock caught the works bus from the factory into Malmesbury and got off at the far end of the town near the Three Cups Inn. Now the hot spell of weather had worsened the beer shortage and this had depressed Jock, He was even more depressed when the Three Cups only allowed him half a pint of beer, Even the regulars were only allowed a pint! So Jock left the pub and ambled back towards the Bell Hotel to try his luck there.

On the way he leant against a garden wall and looked over into the garden and was fascinated with what he saw, although Jock had no interest or love of gardens or gardening. There were very few gardens in that part of Glasgow which Jock called home. However he was intrigued with this garden, there were no flowers and every inch of space was a planted with a plant he did not recognise and all were carefully tended. At this point the front door of the house opened and the occupant seeing Jock said, "Good evening". "Hello", said Jock "What are all these plants". They are parsnips the man said. "You must be very fond of eating parsnips", Jock said. "I don't eat them" the owner replied, "I make wine of them". "Make *wine* with *parsnips*", Jock asked. You had better come in he replied and took Jock into the house and down into a large cellar where there were rows of nine gallon barrels each on its own stand and carefully labelled. There must have been forty or fifty of them. It was cool and airy very different to the smelly pub cellars with which Jock was more familiar. The man poured Jock a generous glass of wine, which he enjoyed. "Here now try some of this ten year old, it is like malt whisky and much stronger".

It was getting dark when Jock left and made his way, unsteadily, down the hill to the Black Horse, our local, where he thought

The Secret War Factory

he might get a nightcap. He walked into the bar and promptly collapsed. Bill, the publican, said "Where the hell did he get the booze to get him into that state". One of the customers who had knelt down beside him said "Its not drink Bill, there is no smell of it". (one of the blessings of parsnip wine apparently) "Someone slip round to the hospital and get a nurse," said Bill. The Cottage Hospital was only just up the road. In a short while a nurse and two porters with a stretcher arrived and Jock was still flat out on the floor. They carried him back to the hospital and kept him in. When the Company enquired at the hospital in the morning they were told he would be discharged at about eleven and had been suffering with too much sun. Anyone knowing Jock knew that his only outdoor activity was walking from pub to pub!!!

As mentioned earlier, electronic valves were supplied by the Ministry and kept in an 'Embodiment Loan Store'. Valves were issued out to Testers and booked to a specific item of equipment. If a valve was faulty it was returned to store and a replacement issued. Now the AI Mk VIII Modulator used three special top-secret valves, glass cylindrical tubes on a metal base 8inches (20cm) tall and 2inches (5cm) in diameter. Some of these valves failed during the 'Tank' Test. On one occasion three new valves were issued but the Store Keeper forgot to ask for the old ones back. The Tester, rather than walk back to the stores with the old ones, just rolled them under the tank and forgot about them.

At stock taking time, some six months later, it was found that the stock of top-secret valves were three short. Of course everybody had forgotten about the incident mentioned earlier, so panic stations. A search was made to no avail. The Tester was adamant that he always took faulty valves to the stores to get replacements and the Storekeeper was equally adamant the he never issued replacement valves without receiving faulty valves. The Management had no alternative but to report it to

Charles Exton

the Ministry who in turn reported it to the local police, little knowing that this was a very small force, and somehow ignoring the tight security that existed at the factory.

The Test Apparatus Department staff were a bunch of enthusiastic Radio Engineers, always thinking up new ideas and they wished for opportunities to experiment in their own time. Greg our senior Radio Engineer had a radio shop down in Somerset but the Ministry of Labour directed him to Malmesbury, as we were so short of Radio Engineers, and his wife, at home, kept the shop ticking over. Greg and Nobby, both keen to have a private workshop managed to rent a small empty shop in Malmesbury for four shillings a week. (Although I worked in the department at that time I did not take part in the project as my spare time was fully taken up in courting the girls!) The rest soon fixed up some permanent black out in the windows and the experimental radio workshop was up and running. The shop in Malmesbury caused a bit of a stir locally because of the permanent black out and men coming and going late at night and on Sundays. When Greg was sent to Malmesbury the Billeting Officer sent him, as he was a mature gentleman, to live in the Manse along with the Bishop.

As mentioned earlier, components and rejected panels from the Salvage Department were heaped up on waste ground and burnt. Many people sorted over this heap and items they thought might be useful were surreptitiously pocketed. At finishing time the mad rush to catch buses etc left the Security Guards little opportunity to search people leaving. Greg, Nobby and the others had a good stock of rejected bits and pieces rescued from the bonfire up in their shop where they were put to good use.

When the Modulator valves went missing and the police were called in, they asked for a Manager from the factory to accompany them in a search of the shop premises, which the

The Secret War Factory

boys had rented, because they could not think of any where else to look for the missing valves. No valves were found, of course, but the Manager identified bits and pieces from the bonfire. "Right" said the police "we will have them for theft", and to the Managers horror, Greg and Nobby were arrested and taken to the police station where they were charged with theft. Greg, as the senior, said that he would take responsibility and he signed a statement saying that he pleaded guilty to taking parts from the factory, which were destined to be burnt. The Manager insisted that the items taken were indeed scrap and the work going on in the shop would ultimately benefit the factory and police action was not necessary but the police were adamant; at least they had a case.

When Greg had time to consider the matter he was concerned that if he had a police record it would not be very good for his business. Greg had been billeted on the Suffragan Bishop of Malmesbury and so he discussed the problem with the Bishop, with whom, by this time, he had become very friendly. The Bishop told him he would get his full support at the hearing. The day of the trial arrived and we were given time off work to attend the hearing. When the charge was read out Greg pleaded 'Not Guilty'. The Police Sergeant stated that he searched the shop accompanied by the Manager and parts were found, as exhibited, that the Manager identified as being Company property and these had been stolen by Greg. He then stated that he had a signed statement where Greg had pleading guilty to the taking parts. The Manager then stated that the parts were scrap and useless to the company and the case should not proceed any further. Greg's solicitor then went into all the details, which were discussed fully. The solicitor certainly spread confusion as he had intended.

Watching the proceedings it was clear that the Magistrates where completely and totally confused – Why would anyone steal useless items which were going to be burnt. Finally the Bishop was called to give Greg a reference, which he did in glowing terms adding that in his house were many small and valuable items and in the two years that Greg had been living there he had never touched a thing and in his view never would because Greg was an honest gentleman. At this point to those watching one could see that the Magistrates were sitting back relieved, for if the Bishop says Greg is a good guy then he is a good guy. The Magistrates retired to discuss the case, which did not take long, and on returning announced "Case Dismissed". A furious Police Sergeant was left thumping the desk and grinding his teeth. We all left cheering.

Some weeks later a diligent cleaner poked her broom handle under the Test Tank, and out rolled three valves. The stock count was now correct and there were almost too many red faces to count.

How did I cope in Malmesbury during the war years? Pretty well I thought except for a lapse in the winter of 1942. I was working on the Teat Apparatus department at that time and we had had a particularly stressful time building, in a rush, the new apparatus for the new AI Mk VIII equipment. We worked till ten in the evening several days in the week and on Sundays as well.

I was living in lodgings at the far end of Malmesbury and used to catch the works bus at seven thirty in the morning to be at work at work at eight o'clock. It was always a rush, eating bread and margarine and drinking tea standing up in order to catch the bus.

One morning I revolted, sat down and took my time as I knew the staff bus left at eight ten to be at the works at eight thirty, the staff's starting time. This bus took less time because there

The Secret War Factory

were less pick up points. I continued to go on the later bus each morning and it wasn't long before my manager noticed my lateness and duly gave me a lecture, which I ignored and carried on as before. At his second lecture he told me I would be reported to the Personnel Manager. The lecture from him was also ignored. At the second confrontation I was told I would be reported to the Tribunal, whatever that was.

Eventually I received a letter from the Ministry of Labour ordering me to attend a Disciplinary Tribunal at the Council Offices in Malmesbury on the following Wednesday at three o'clock. I enjoyed the walk too Malmesbury in the daylight as it had been dark mornings and evenings for some time. On the way I considered what I should say to the Tribunal. I didn't think they would buy the truth which was I was tired and depressed. Then I remembered someone told me that he was unable to get his alarm clock repaired or but a new one. So, that would be my story.

The Tribunal consisted of a representative of the Ministry of Labour in Bristol a senior Trade's Union Official, also from Bristol. A local magistrate, a local doctor, and a local priest. I was severely lectured about my persistent lateness at work and the importance of war work. I was the asked for an explanation. I gave my excuses about the alarm clock. I was asked if my landlady called me in the morning. I said "No". A policeman was sent round to interview my landlady and when asked if she called me in the morning she said "No" adding" if he wants to be late at work that is his business not mine". After the policeman had delivered his message, I was asked to leave the room while the matter was being considered.

On my return I was told that an alarm clock would be available for me to purchase from the local jewellers within a week and I would be fined £5-00. If I appeared before them again the results would be more serious, probably with my being transferred to the armed forces where their discipline would ensure that I was uo early in the morning.

On my walk back to the factory I smarted over the £5-00 but decided that I did my like my work and that I would just have to pull myself together and catch the eight o'clock bus but oh, I enjoyed the short respite from the routine and long hours which dragged down everybody at one time or another.

APPENDIX
Now it can be told

By the outbreak of war in September 1939 we had 20 operational Radar Stations from Scotland to the Isle of Wight, each with a range of about 170 miles, By February 1940 32 stations covered the whole of the coastline of England, Wales and Scotland, with small gaps on the west coast of Scotland. Airborne Radar was also becoming well established. Work on the development of airborne radar was also proceeding.

It cannot be said that Radar won the war but it did stop us from loosing it! Ground Radar at first detected incoming aircraft as the coastal radar was 'looking' out to sea and the operators could contact Fighter Command informing them of the position of the incoming enemy. Inevitably some aircraft got through and we didn't know where they were. A second chain of radar stations was set up named GCI (Ground control interception) and it was their job to locate these aircraft that had crossed the coast and direct fighter aircraft to intercept them.

As early as 1936 thoughts were being given to the possibilities of Airborne Radar. How could it be conceived considering that a ground Radar transmitter occupied a whole room and weighed many tons? Nevertheless some sort of a specification was compiled; it must not occupy a space of more than 8 cubic feet, not weigh more than 200 pounds and not use more than 500 watts of electrical power.

What an order. However progress was made. EMI had developed a straight TRF Television operating on 45 Mc/s, the BBC TV broadcasting frequency. This was lightweight and compact and be suitable for a 7.6 metre radar receiver. What was needed now was a small lightweight pulse transmitter operating on 7.6 metre wavelength (45 Mc/s). Eventually such a transmitter was built using Western Electric 316A valves 'Giant Acorns'. The pulse recurrence was about 1000 per second and the pulse width 2 or 3 microseconds, but the power output would not have been much more than a couple of hundred watts. This set up was installed in a Heyford Bomber in March 1937 and flown up the East Coast. Clear signals were received for prominent objects on the ground, particularly from dock cranes. Also there were distinct echoes in the distance, which could have come from ships. Flushed with this success, it was decided to concentrate on ASV (Air to Surface Vessel) as ships offered a much larger target that aircraft.

It was decided to lower the wavelength to 1.5 metres. This was achieved by making the receiver a superhet by using American acorn valves as a local oscillator and a mixer and the 45 Mc/s Receiver as an Intermediate Amplifier. From then on 45Mc/s remained the Standard Intermediate Frequency for all airborne radar systems. Towards the end of 1938 contracts were placed for 6 receivers from Cossor and 6 transmitters from Metro-Vickers. These contractors were chosen because both had built the ground Radar Equipment. The contractors were shown the models and were given specifications. Six months later Cossor delivered six receivers, which were a complete failure, the sensitivity was too low and there was no means of increasing it and their weight was more than the original complete system. Metro-Vickers delivered nothing at all.

In April 1939 it was found that Pye Radio had also built a TRF TV Receiver similar to EMI. Samples were obtained and the results were superior to the EMI model. Pye had used the Mullard EF 50 valve; later it was to become the VR91. Within a few weeks Pye had produced the complete 200 Mc/s receiver using the same acorn valves. E.K.Cole was brought in to produce the transmitters using the VT 90 'micro pup' valves made by GEC at Wembley. These units with a Display Unit became ASV Mark I.

At a meeting on June 11th 1939, the authority was granted for the development of AI equipment to be accorded the highest priority in view of the poor state of the Country's night defences. Following the completion of the first batch of AI sets the Air Ministry decided to develop a production version under the designation AI Mk II. Work on the Mk II system began in October 1939, with responsibility for the development of improved Transmitters and Receivers being allocated to E.K.Cole and Pye Radio respectively. The first Mk II sets were installed in a Blenheim in January 1940

The design of the new Transmitters by E.K.Cole's Western Development Unit (W.D.U.) was located in a group of buildings in Malmesbury High Street next door to Lloyds Bank. Most of the Staff and Engineers lived in a large Country House, The Priory, which had been converted into a hostel. The Priory was located in the Chippenham Road just beyond the Silk Mill and very conveniently opposite the Black Horse Inn.

The Black Horse was the favourite watering hole for most of W.D.U and the Factory Employees. Bill Jones, the Landlord made us all very welcome in contrast to our reception in the other pubs in the town. As a result Bill was busy every evening of the week whereas the other pubs relied on weekend trade.

The resulting friction this caused between Bill Jones and the other Landlords caused them to vote Bill off the Local Licensed Victualler's Association. Bill did not worry and cried all the way to the Bank!

The main difference between ASV and AI was that with ASV only a range display was required, measuring the distance of ships from the aircraft, whereas with AI Azimuth Distance as well as Range was required in order to locate an aircraft. Range was dependant on aircraft height and at 15,000 feet the maximum range would be about three miles, but at 10,000 feet the range was less than two miles, which did not leave much room for manoeuvre. Methods were tried to display azimuth position but most of these reduced the maximum range to an unacceptable figure. The system adopted was of the kind well known in the Lorentz landing system shown below.

This illustration shows the overlapping aerial patterns in (a) Azimuth and (b) Elevation of 200MHz air-interception Radar

The illustration below shows the display on the two cathode Ray tubes

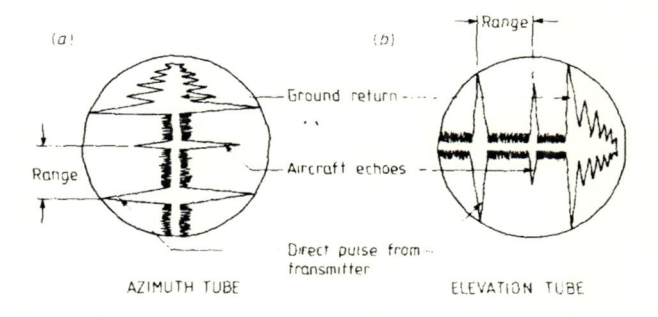

```
      (a)                    (b)              ├─Range─┤
                        ─Ground return
                        ─Aircraft echoes
  Range
                        Direct pulse from
                        transmitter
   AZIMUTH TUBE                              ELEVATION TUBE
```

Coping with two separate aerial systems meant considerable change to the receiver input. A motor driven switch was devised to switch first one aerial system to the receiver and then the other in rapid succession. Also two display cathode ray tubes were required. The display on the left shows the transmitter pulse A, the target B and the ground return C. The distance A – B gives the range, and the relative sizes of the blips above and below of the median line shows the target is below the fighter. Similarly the display on the right shows that the target is on the right of the fighter. As the fighter catches up with the target the blips slide down towards the transmitter pulse until it finally disappears into the transmitter pulse. This sets the minimum range at which a target would be visible.

It became clear that there was a need for further improvement to the AI's performance. The AI Mk II transmitter was abandoned and replaced by that of ASV Mk I. This system was successfully used by Coastal Command to search for German vessels planting mines on British Coastal Waters. This equipment demonstrated in maximum range to 17,000 feet (5.180 metres). Further changes to the transmitter for AI use reduced this minimum range to 600 feet (180 metres). This system was designated AI Mk III, however it was dogged with many problems and did not achieve much operational success. The Transmitter however, was a particularly useful unit and found a number of other uses as in the Naval 272 installation, the Army AMES 6 installation and in the SLC (Elsie) Searchlight Control System.

The main problem with AI Mk III and earlier radars was that they failed to see the target at the short enough ranges suitable for accurate gunfire because the radar echo would merge with the transmitter pulse.

Taking AI Mark III as a basis, a team from EMI under the leadership of A.D.Blumlein was awarded a contract in May 1940 to design a radar based on their separate Modulator system. The Mark III's self modulating transmitter was replaced by one controlled by pulses generated by a separate modulator unit. This apparatus overcame the minimum range problem. An additional control was provided for the radar operator to adjust the back edge of the direct pulse to a point where it was visible on his CRT (Cathode Ray Tube). This principle of operation was subsequently adopted on all 1.5 metre radars. The display units and the receiver were the same or very similar to those used on AI Mk III.

The new system, designated AI MK IV flew for the first time in June 1940 and immediately showed itself to be a great improvement on the AI Mark III. An initial problem was the instability of the echoes on the indicator unit's CRTs. Modifications were made and further trials in July were able to confirm that new set demonstrated a lower minimum range and improved maximum range compared to AI mark III. This gave the RAF their first practical AI Radar Set.

RAF Beaufighters equipped with AI Mark IV Radar
January 1941 3 Kills   February 1941 4 Kills
March 1941   22 Kills   April 1941   45 Kills
May 1941   over 100 Kills

It took time for the air crew to become familiar with the new equipment, and particularly, for pilots to become accustomed to act upon navigational directions given to them by their radar operators who alone new the location of their target.

Successful as AI MK IV was, one problem was that there was a tendency for night-fighters to 'weave' from side to side as they approached the target. It was concluded that this was caused by the time lag in the passing of information from the operator to his pilot. It was considered that this could be overcome if the later part of the interception was controlled solely by the pilot. One solution was the provision of a pilot's indicator in the cockpit. Thus AI Mk V came into being.

Even now, development of AI Mk VI was underway. The equipment, fitted with a 'wandering' strobe, (this was a bright spot on the screen over the target signal to distinguish it from other signals) and was completely automatic in operation. Since it required no operator it was suitable for installation in single-seat fighters. The set functioned similarly to AI Mk V, excepting the strobing function, which was carried out automatically to drive the pilot's indicator. A prototype installation was fitted into a Hurricane in March 1942. Technically the trials were a success, but by this time experiments with centimetric wavelengths looked likely to seriously challenge 1.5 metre radars. For this reason AI Mk VI became obsolete almost before it became fitted into fighters in any quantity. Manufacturing quantities were reduced and many of the surplus sets were modified and fitted into Bomber Aircraft as tail warning radars, alerting the crew of the approach of enemy fighters from the rear.

By now the development of AI MK VII was seriously underway. The development of the Magnetron at Birmingham University which produced a pulsed output 10 kW on a wavelength of less than 10 cms meant that airborne radar would now be capable of operating at low altitudes and with a smaller minimum range than was possible at a 1.5 metre wavelength. There were other new innovations. A dipole aerial common to both transmitter and receiver was introduced and a new device know as a 'T.R Switch' was developed and fitted to the receiver. This prevented the transmitter pulse entering the receiver whilst still permitting the weak echo pulses through. Another innovation was the aerial dish some 28 inches (70.1cm) in diameter. which eccentrically revolved at high speed giving an overall beam angle of +/- 45 degrees. The indicator now had a single cathode ray tube and due to rotation of the aerial dish gave a spiral scan. If the operator saw a portion of a circular scan at twelve o'clock on his indicator then the target is somewhere above him. If the arc appeared at three o'clock it is at the same height as he is but somewhere to starboard. If the pilot now turns to starboard then the arc on the tube will grow larger and when it appears as a full circle he will be right behind the target. Now the distance from the target is shown be the distance of the arc or circle from the centre of the tube so as that distance gets smaller so is the distance from the target reducing. See chapter 17 to see how AI MK VIII was handled at Malmesbury.

Some bus drivers brought children in to meet their parents and ride back home with them – photo from the D Grainger collection

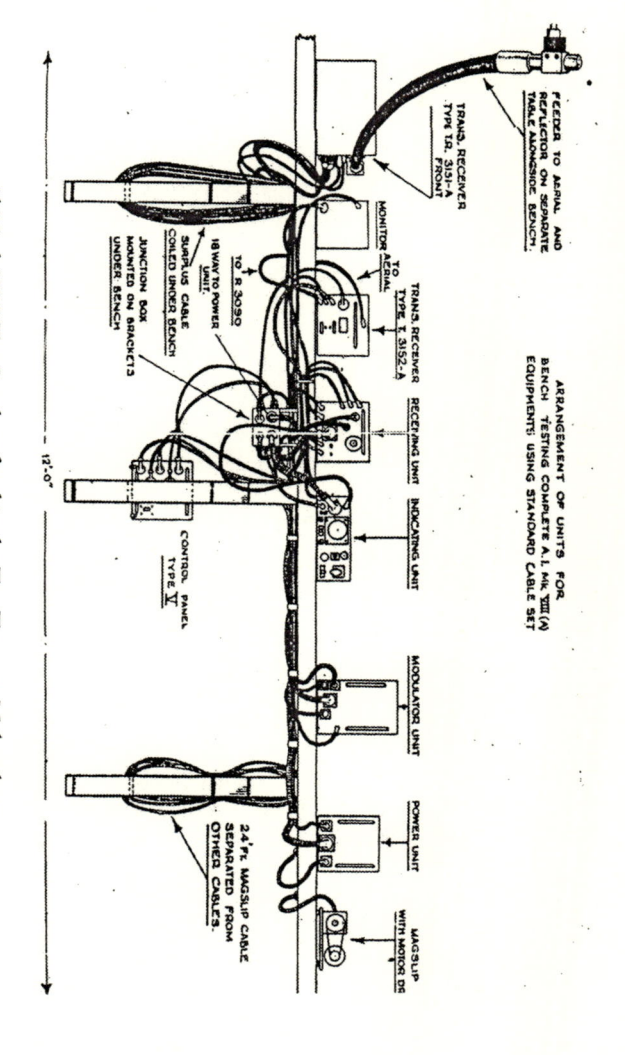

AI Mark VIII Test Bench as fitted in the Test Tower at Malmesbury.

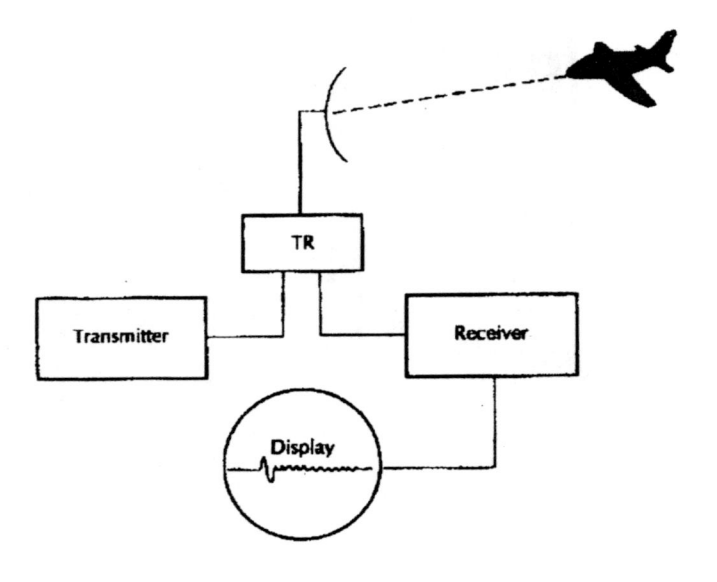

The transmitter pulse goes out at intervals and in the time between these pulses, the small pulses from the targets pass to the receiver through the TR switch. This eliminates any "breakthrough" from the transmitter to the receiver.

The transmitter pulse goes out at intervals through the TR switch.

During the intervals between transmitter pulses, the small pulses from the target arrives at the receiver through the TR switch. This eliminates any breakthrough from the transmitter pulse into the receiver.

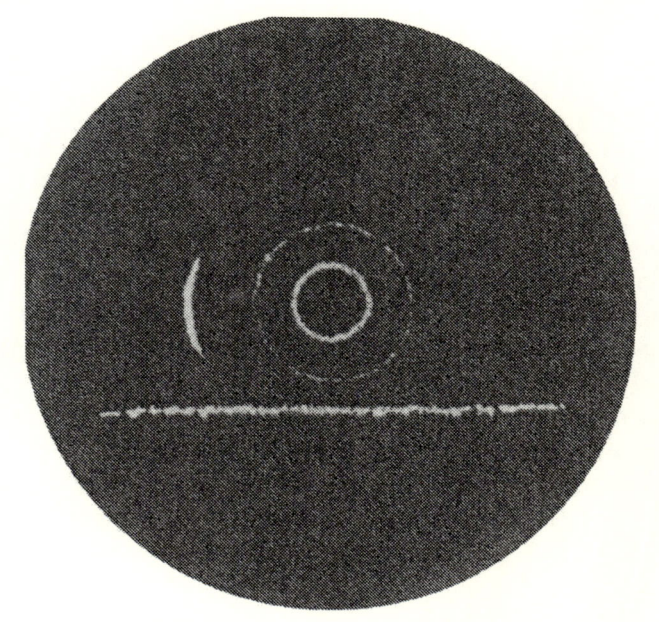

The display of the AI Mark VIII system

The new de Havilland Mosquito was a twin engined, two seat, cantilever monoplane built almost entirely of wood. The engines were 12 cylinder, liquid cooled, Rolls-Royce Merlins, developing 1,230 hp., which gave a maximum speed of 380 mph (610 km/hr) at 13,000 feet (3960 Metres). It flew easily on one engine. Built as a bomber it, was adapted as a high performance day and night fighter capable of reaching deep into Germany.

The pilot occupied the left hand seat with the radar operator on the right and slightly behind, with the AI Mk VIII indicator immediately in front of him. This was the aircraft and radar system, which was such a successful combination.

In early 1943 the design of a new system to be designated AI Mk IX was to proceed. But progress was slow because of so much time and effort spent putting AI Mk VIII into service. At this time Churchill had authorized bomber command to use Window. Window was a system consisting of lengths of aluminium foil cut into lengths matching the wavelength of German radars and when bundles of these were dropped, German radars were tricked into seeing many thousands of false radar echoes and assumed a large bomber attack was imminent. Churchill's reluctance to allow the use of Window was that the Germans would retaliate and use it on us and the effect on our defence system was unknown. It was then realised the AI MK IX would have to operate on a different wavelength to that of AI MK VIII in fact at 3 cms. It became evident that this new system could not be produced in any quantity before the end of the war. As the American System SCR 720 was available and showed discrimination under Window jamming and better overall coverage and increased maximum range over AI MKVIII it was decided to abandon the development of AI MK IX.

Thus SCR 720 was imported in large quantities however modifications were required to make them suitable for use by the RAF and they were then known as AI MK X. These modifications were carried out in this country largely by E.K.Cole in the factory in Malmesbury. AI MK X had many new features. It was the first airborne radar equipment to have the units fitted into pressurised containers. This of course reduced the problems of high voltage flashovers and they were now operating in a constant environment and not affected by changes in altitude. First installations were commenced in December 1943 and the first 'kill' was a Ju 188 shot down over Essex in February 1944. This was the last AI equipment before the end of the war however; AI MK X remained in service until the late 50s.

AI Mark X (SCR 720) Test Bench

ABBREVIATIONS

AI   Air Interception Radar. A radar installation in fighter aircraft to detect and intercept enemy aircraft

ASV   Air to Surface vessel. An Airborne Radar for the diction of ships and surfaced submarines.

TRF   Tuned Radio Frequency Amplifier. Early TV receivers were of this type, also referred to as straight sets.

DEFINITIONS

Frequency and Wavelength

Frequency is the number of times the crest of a radio wave passes a given point, measured in Kc/s = 1,000 times per second. or Mc/.s = 1,000,000 times per second.

Wavelength is the distance in metres from the crest of one wave to the crest of the next. For Radio Waves it is equal in metres to 300,000 ÷ Frequency in Kc/s. Thus a wavelength of 1.5 metres = frequency of 200 Mc/s or a Frequency of 45 Mc/s = wavelength of 6.7 metres.

REFERENCES

Permission has been granted to publish extracts from the Mass-Observation Report 'The War Factory', by the Trustees of the Mass-Observation Archive.

Unless otherwise stated, photos used have been supplied by Chris Poole, historian to www.ekco-radar.co.uk, which is a website dedicated to recording and preserving the history of radar and communications Manufacture at Ekco.

Public Records Office Files:

AIR	29/27
AIR	10/5485
AIR	10/3988
AVIA 7	1092
	1398
	1712 D1786
	1875
	1975
	1978
	2022
	2627

AVIA10	3988
	4018
AVIA13	1047
	1050
AVIA 26	308
	1114
AP	2551A
AP	2913

Printed in the United Kingdom
by Lightning Source UK Ltd.
125153UK00001B/1/A